SEVEN STEPS TO TRAIN YOUR MIND

Seven Steps
to Train
Your Mind

Gomo Tulku

Translation of Gomo Tulku's
"Annotations to the Foundational Verses
for Training the Mind"
(Blo sbyong rtsa tshig la mchan 'grel)
and edition of the oral commentary by

Joan Nicell

WISDOM PUBLICATIONS · BOSTON

Wisdom Publications
199 Elm Street
Somerville, MA 02144 USA
www.wisdompubs.org

Library of Congress Cataloging-in-Publication Data
Gomo Tulku, 1922–1985.
  [Becoming a child of the Buddhas]
  Seven steps to train your mind / Gomo Tulku ; translation of Gomo Tulku's "Annotations to the Foundational Verses for Training the Mind" (Blo sbyong rtsa tshig la mchan 'grel) and edition of the oral commentary by Joan Nicell.
      pages cm
  Previously published under title: Becoming a child of the Buddhas : a simple clarification of the Root verses of seven point mind training, c1998.
  Includes bibliographical references and index.
  ISBN 1-61429-226-4 (alk. paper)
    1. Ye-ses-rdo-rje, 'Chad-kha-ba, 1102–1176. Blo sbyon don bdun ma. 2. Blo-Bzan-'jam-dbyans-smon-lam, Ke'u-tshan Sprul-sku, active 18th century. Blo sbyon rtsa tshig. 3. Spiritual life—Bka'-gdams-pa (Sect) 4. Dge-lugs-pa (Sect)—Doctrines. I. Ye-ses-rdo-rje, 'Chad-kha-ba, 1102–1176. Blo sbyon don bdun ma. II. Blo-bzan-'jam-dbyans-smon-lam, Ke'u-tshan Sprul-sku, active 18th century. Blo sbyon rtsa tshig. English. III. Title.
  BQ7670.6.G67 2015
  294.3'444—dc23

                        2014035072

ISBN 978-1-61429-226-5   ebook ISBN 978-0-86171-900-6

19 18 17 16 15   5 4 3 2 1

CONTENTS

FOREWORD

BY THE TWENTY-THIRD GOMO TULKU, TENZIN D. KASHHI

I WAS BORN in Canada in 1988 and for the early years of my life lived in Canada and the United States. From the age of seven until I was nineteen I lived and studied at one of the biggest Tibetan monasteries in India. It was difficult for me, growing up in these parallel worlds, to find a place in which to be truly at peace. Over time I have come to the conclusion, based on personal experience and investigation, that there is no better place in which to find authentic peace than in my own mind. I had only myself to blame if my peace was threatened. In short, we can't expect to find peace somewhere outside of ourselves in the external world.

One of the things I have found most useful from my study of Buddhist philosophy is its understanding of the psychology that underlies peoples' happiness and unhappiness. From the point of view of my recent experiences as a recording artist in the music scene, I can say that people are generally driven by the hype of pop culture and easily influenced by the names and faces that govern many aspects of social status. While this is fine to a certain degree, we can sometimes get wrapped up in the feeling that we "gotta match up," which jeopardizes our own happiness and inner peace. The need to have the same shoes as the person we see on television or the feeling that we don't look good because some model looks better makes us unhappy by making us discontent with what we have or who we are. Therefore, to me, the main keys to building some peace of mind are to be aware of our minds, to come to know the value of our lives, and to cultivate a sense of genuine contentment.

A sense of contentment can come about in many ways. It may be that when we watch the news and see all the genocide going on in the world, it puts our own problems in perspective and helps us see how lucky we are to live in a place where we can say what we want and sing about the way we feel without fear that the system will clamp down and punish us. Looking at the problems that make us unhappy from a broader perspective can help us to see that these are often not real problems compared to what many people in the world experience. Understanding that others have much bigger problems than ours can help us get over the "gotta match up" mindset so that we feel less unsettled by material and status competition.

I'm glad that you've read these few words, because it means that you are about to embark on a journey that will give you the tools you need to better understand how your own mind works. Pursuing the practice of training your mind will be of benefit to yourself and others because you will develop a greater awareness of your own states of mind and understand how to put your mind to good use. I wish you every success on your journey.

Tenzin D. Kashhi
The Twenty-Third Gomo Tulku
Pomaia, Italy
July 2014

FOREWORD

BY LAMA THUBTEN ZOPA RINPOCHE

TO WHOEVER READS this precious holy Dharma text, I would like to mention how extremely fortunate you are to have this opportunity to receive the precious holy teachings of guru Gomo Rinpoche, whose kindness is greater than that of all the past, present, and future buddhas.

Rinpoche once wrote me a letter from his home in Mussorie, India, telling me that he had hopes of definitely becoming enlightened in his very lifetime. This statement implies that Rinpoche's mind had become one with the practice; in other words, his mind had become one with devotion to the guru (the root of the path to enlightenment), as well as renunciation, the mind of enlightenment (bodhicitta), the wisdom realizing emptiness, and the two stages of tantra. It means that he had attained the realizations of clear light and illusory body because, without these realizations, he could not have said that he hoped to become enlightened in his lifetime.

In fact, it was obvious to us disciples that Rinpoche's teachings on tantra came from his own personal experience, and, in spite of our ordinary obscured way of perceiving things, we could still see that he had incredible qualities. As a result of his subdued mind and his realizations, his teachings immediately subdued the minds of his listeners. Just as snow naturally melts in the heat of the sun and butter melts on a hot pan, his teachings, due to his wisdom and compassion, naturally cooled, or pacified, our disturbed emotional minds.

The topic of the teachings contained in this book is mind training, or thought transformation, which is the most profound form of psychology and the best form of meditation. The teachings on mind training explain how to integrate our daily life experiences with meditation and Dharma practice, especially when we experience problems and our minds are filled with disturbing emotions. The mind training teachings show us how to make our lives beneficial even in times of difficulty by using problems as the path to enlightenment, the highest happiness. Through thought transformation practice—the application of either the ultimate mind of enlightenment, the realization of emptiness, or the conventional mind of enlightenment, the thought to achieve enlightenment for the benefit of all sentient beings—we can transform the experience of any difficulty (relationship problems, cancer, AIDS, and even our own death) into a cause for all sentient beings' happiness. In other words, not only do our sufferings become the cause of our own happiness, they also become the cause of countless other sentient beings' happiness. Through practicing mind training we can transform even the experience of problems into something extremely beneficial and useful for other sentient beings.

Mind training allows us to use problems as a method

to purify our mental obscurations and the negative actions we committed in the past. Through developing the mind of enlightenment, we will also simultaneously accumulate merit similar in extent to the infinite sky. Thus, through the practice of transforming our minds, problems become a quick path to enlightenment.

Because Rinpoche himself lived the practice of mind training, his teachings come from experience and are not just empty words. For this reason, we are extremely fortunate to have this opportunity to study his teachings and to put into practice whatever we have understood.

I hope and pray that numberless sentient beings have the chance to read this book and thereby plant the seeds of liberation and enlightenment in their minds. May they achieve enlightenment as quickly as possible.

Kopan Monastery, Nepal
November 1995

PREFACE

WHEN WE EXPERIENCE adversity, our tendency is to point to people and conditions external to ourselves as the source of all our problems. Consequently, during difficult periods in our lives we tend to find fault in everyone we meet, even in our friends and relatives. In contrast, when we apply specific methods for training our mind, we practice looking inside ourselves for the reasons we are experiencing hardship. As we do so, we eventually discover that we alone are responsible for all our problems. This is because the reason behind all our problems is that we have not been taking care of our own minds. Instead, we have allowed our minds to run wild under the control of the three mental poisons of attachment, hatred, and ignorance. If instead we carefully examine the source of our problems, we will come to the conclusion that not a single problem is caused by conditions external to our own mind. On further investigation, we will also come to realize that, due to having familiarized ourselves with the mental poisons during our many past lives, we will continue to experience suffering in this and all our future lives—if we do not take action against those poisons right now.

The main reason we are unable to take care of our minds

and apply the antidotes, or remedies, to the three mental poisons is our strong tendency to cherish ourselves above all others. This tendency shows itself in a variety of ways, such as how we hold our bodies and our belongings to be so precious. However, in my own experience, the most harmful of selfish attitudes is that of being happy and pleased with the people who help or praise us and being unhappy and angry with the people who speak harshly to us or criticize us. These feelings bring about attachment to the resulting "friends," and anger toward the resulting "enemies." These negative emotions, which are the result of cherishing ourselves, totally destroy our mental happiness and make us confused. If, on the contrary, we were able to view other people and their actions with equanimity, we would discover real peace of mind.

Generally speaking, when other people treat us well, we have a tendency to feel pleased and gratified. Having practiced the methods for training the mind, I can honestly say that I no longer have this reaction when, for example, people show me respect or offer things to me. Now, even when people treat me disrespectfully or do not help me, I can remain very relaxed and peaceful, without unhappy or negative thoughts toward them.

In fact, the reason that I have chosen to teach this particular topic, the practice of mind training, is because I have personally experienced its great benefit. In 1948, I experienced a period of great personal hardship and difficulty. I was very unhappy and felt frustrated and tense. I therefore began to look for some means to bring my mind back under control, to regain a state of mental tranquility. I discovered that the only way for me to remain happy was to engage in the practices collectively known as "mind training," or *lojong* in Tibetan. I read many texts on this subject and, at the same time, I tried to put these methods into practice. Through doing so, I was eventually able to bring my mind back under control, and thereby regain inner peace and contentment. Then, to remind myself of the mind training practices, I wrote a commentary to Geshe Chekawa's mind training text, *Seven-Point Mind Training* (*Blo sbyong don bdun ma*), based on my own experience.

Later on, as a refugee in India in 1962, I once again experienced a difficult period. As before, I turned to the practice of mind training and read many texts written on this subject by the great yogis of the past. I then rewrote my commentary on *Seven-Point Mind Training*, the original version having been lost when I fled Tibet. My commentary, *Annotations to Foundational Verses for Training the Mind*, was subsequently checked and amended by the junior tutor of His Holiness the Dalai Lama, Kyabje Trijang Rinpoche.

My hope is that these teachings on training the mind will also be of benefit to you, whenever you too experience mental and physical problems.

Gomo Tulku
Istituto Lama Tzong Khapa
Pomaia, Italy
February 1985

EDITOR'S ACKNOWLEDGMENTS

I EXTEND my heartfelt gratitude to my spiritual guide and precious teacher, Geshe Jampa Gyatso, for his patient help in translating Gomo Rinpoche's *Annotations to Foundational Verses for Training the Mind*, which was written in a colloquial Tibetan largely unfamiliar to me.

Many thanks to Denis Huet, former director of Institut Vajra Yogini, Lavaur, France, for his kind permission to include the oral commentary on *Annotations to Foundational Verses for Training the Mind* given by Gomo Tulku at that center affiliated with the Foundation for the Preservation of the Mahayana Tradition (FPMT) in April 1985.

I also extend my thanks to Dyanna Cridelich for her excellent work in transcribing the oral commentaries that form the basis of this book, and to John Dunne, of Wisdom Publications, for his invaluable editorial comments.

I would also like to express my appreciation to Massimo Stordi (Gelong Thubten Tsognyi), a devoted disciple of the late Gomo Tulku and former director of Istituto Lama Tzong Khapa, for suggesting I work on preparing this text for publication, thus giving me an opportunity to study and reflect on the practice of training the mind.

My very deep gratitude to Andrew Francis, of Wisdom

Publications, for giving me another precious opportunity to review the teachings in this book, which so clearly set out the essence of the practices for training the mind. Sixteen years after the publication of the first edition of this book, I have even more respect for the profundity of these teachings, so simply set out, yet so difficult to put into practice. May I and everyone else become free from a self-centered attitude and develop the altruistic mind concerned about others' happiness every moment of the day.

A NOTE ON THE TEXT

THERE EXIST SEVERAL slightly different redactions of *Seven-Point Mind Training,* also known as *Foundational Verses for Training the Mind.* They differ in the order in which the lines of the text are presented (the training in the absolute enlightened attitude of bodhicitta in particular occurs toward the beginning in some redactions and toward the end in others), in how the lines of the text are parsed into the seven points, and in the addition and omission of various lines. The version included here matches the source text for Gomo Tulku's *Annotations to Foundational Verses for Training the Mind.*

In order to understand the structure of this book, the reader needs to be aware that it contains the translations of two Tibetan texts along with the transcript of an oral explanation given by Gomo Tulku to these texts. The main or root text is *Seven-Point Mind Training* by Kadam geshe Chekawa; this text appears in bold-face, sans-serif type throughout this book. Gomo Tulku's own concise written commentary to this text, which he called *Annotations to Foundational Verses for Training the Mind,* appears after the lines of the *Seven-Point Mind Training* and is indented, set in sans-serif type throughout. These two texts are followed by the unindented transcript of Gomo Tulku's oral explanation of the texts, in which he further elaborates on their meaning. Although this structure may at times result in a bit of repetition, it is a common way of teaching in the Tibetan tradition and is meant to drive a point home. Because the teachings of the Buddha are not simply for the purpose of gaining mere knowledge, but are intended to bring about a profound and lasting change in our way of thinking and acting, repetition serves as a time-tested method for helping us to remember what it is we need to do!

The translation of *Annotations to Foundational Verses for Training the Mind* by Gomo Tulku is based on an earlier English translation by Thubten Jampa and George Churinoff (Gelong Thubten Tsultrim) and an Italian translation by Massimo Stordi (Gelong Thubten Tsognyi). The oral commentary by Gomo Tulku included in this volume was created by merging a brief teaching that he gave on *Annotations* at Istituto Lama Tzong Khapa, Pomaia, Italy, in February of 1985 and a more extensive teaching that he gave at Institut Vajra Yogini, Lavaur, France, in April of 1985.

SEVEN STEPS TO TRAIN THE MIND

INTRODUCTION

ALL THE BUDDHA'S TEACHINGS can be considered methods or techniques for training the mind—that is, for transforming the mind from a general state of nonvirtue to one of virtue, from self-centeredness to altruism, and from having an unreliable perspective on reality to having a reliable one. Just as repeated efforts to increase strength, flexibility, and endurance train the physical body, so too do repeated efforts to transform negative mental states into positive ones train the mind. In this sense, we can think of the cultivation of ethical discipline, meditative concentration, and wisdom[1] that the Buddha prescribes as forms of mind training.

However, the practice of training the mind that is dealt with in this book refers more precisely to those practices that specifically develop and enhance the two aspects of the enlightened attitude of *bodhicitta*: the relative enlightened attitude—an altruistic aspiration to achieve buddhahood, the state of complete awakening, for the sake of our fellow living beings—and the absolute enlightened attitude—the wisdom that clearly and directly realizes that we ourselves and the world we live in lack any type of ultimately real, enduring, and independent existence. These two attitudes, synthesized as compassion and wisdom, are likened to the wings of a bird: using both of them together we can quickly soar to enlightenment[2] and can become buddhas. Because enlightenment is the goal at the heart of Mahāyāna, or "Universal Vehicle," Buddhism, it is the focus of all the meditations, prayers, and practices that bodhisattvas, those who use the Universal Vehicle, undertake. Thus the practice of mind training taught in this particular book epitomizes the path of Mahāyāna Buddhism.

Among the many texts on mind training that have been written in Tibet over the centuries, the most well-known are probably the *Eight Verses for Training the Mind*[3] written by Langri Thangpa (1054–1153), a master of the Kadam school of Tibetan Buddhism, and *Seven-Point Mind Training* written by Geshe Chekawa (1101–75), a later master of the same school. All mind training texts in general, and *Seven-Point Mind Training* in particular, are thought to take their lead from a compilation of sayings called *Foundational Lines for Training the Mind*. This work has been attributed to Dīpaṃkara Śrījñāna (982–1054), more widely known as Atiśa, an Indian scholar-monk who spent the last seventeen years of his life teaching in Tibet and who founded the Kadam School.

Atiśa passed the mind training teachings to his main Tibetan disciple Dromtönpa. They were then handed down through the Kadam masters Potowa, Langri Thangpa, and Sharawa, until they reached Chekawa, who compiled them in the *Seven-Point Mind Training*.[4] The transmission of the study and practice of this text continued uninterruptedly from guru to disciple all the way down to Gomo Tulku, who in 1985 taught this text to audiences first in Italy and then in France. That *Seven-Point Mind Training* is still widely taught in all four schools of the Tibetan Buddhist tradition and that there are a growing number of contemporary commentaries available on it attests to the fact that the mind training practices are as useful today as they were almost a thousand years ago, when Atiśa first taught the subject to his Tibetan disciples.

What characterizes the mind training texts in general? They propose a radical change—a complete 180° turn about—from our present self-centered ways of thinking about and perceiving ourselves and the world we live in. These texts teach us how to replace an attitude that holds ourselves to be more important than everyone else with an attitude that cherishes others first and foremost. Developing a compassionate attitude that wishes to attain enlightenment in order to relieve the suffering of all sentient beings is the greatest expression of altruism. To achieve this we must first have a healthy sense of our own value and potential as intelligent and good-hearted human beings— in other words, a *healthy* sense of self-importance. Understanding the great value and potential that our own lives possess and seeing that this value exists within each of our fellow living beings, we can then begin the work of bringing about the fundamental transformation of all of our thoughts and actions by training our minds.

The Kadam masters thought of religiously inclined people as naturally belonging to three classes based on their motivations for spiritual practice: those who have a lesser motivation, who practice Dharma based on the wish to enter a happy realm after death; those who have a middling motivation, who practice Dharma based on the wish to wholly escape from the misery of existence; and those who have the greatest motivation, who practice Dharma based on the wish to free all living beings from suffering and lead them to the final peace of complete enlightenment. In *Seven-Point Mind Training* Geshe Chekawa instructs us to begin our practice with "the preliminaries," which include the meditations for people who have lesser and middling motivations and are the first step in training our minds. The preliminary meditations comprise the foundation for meditations practiced by people who have the greatest motivation—those who undertake Buddhist practices motivated by the enlightened attitude of bodhicitta.[5]

By familiarizing ourselves with the meditations undertaken with the lesser motivation, we gradually shift our focus from just seeking happiness in this life to seeking happiness beyond this life. To obtain happiness in future lives we must take refuge in the Three Jewels—the Buddha, Dharma, and Sangha—and observe the law of actions and their consequences—avoiding nonvirtuous behavior and always striving to act virtuously. Based on these meditations, we then contemplate the suffering that pervades *samsara*[6] in general, including even the best states of life that one can attain therein. By meditating on the drawbacks of cyclic existence, we come to understand that even a good future rebirth will be no guarantee of lasting happiness. As long as we continue to circle from life to life in the cycle of existence, driven by our actions and mental affliction,[7] we will always encounter suffering. When we give up chasing after mediocre happiness and develop the wish to escape from the unsatisfactory states of cyclic existence altogether for the enduring happiness of nirvana, we have developed a middling motivation. Guided by this motivation we undertake to practice the three higher trainings in ethics, meditative concentration, and wisdom.

But how can we be satisfied with freeing only ourselves, when innumerable other living beings continue to suffer in the cycle of existence? Shouldn't we do something to help them? Having reflected on the sad state of our fellow living beings who also suffer as they circle from birth to birth, we develop a heartfelt wish to become someone capable of freeing them from suffering and leading them to the enduring peace of enlightenment. With this greater sense of responsibility for others our practice becomes one based on the greatest possible motivation.

So how do we develop this great motivation in such a way that it will become the stable bedrock required to sustain a course of practice that will likely span many lifetimes before we realize our goal? This is the central topic of Geshe Chekawa's *Seven-Point Mind Training*.

At the heart of the practice of training the mind is a mindset that consistently recognizes our mistaken sense of self and inflated sense of self-importance[8] as the sources of the mental afflictions that bind us in the cycle of existence. Although we innately feel that we, as characterized by the notion "I," are special or more important than anyone else, this attitude is inherently flawed because it is based on the mistaken feeling that we somehow really and truly exist as enduring and uncompounded selves—something more than the fleeting assemblage of bodies and minds. The Buddha recognized this mistaken sense of self as the fundamental type of ignorance that is the source of our wandering through life after life in the cycle of existence; if we eliminate that ignorance we will cease to wander and come to rest in the peace of nirvana. However, if we were to not only eliminate the basic ignorance that traps us in the cycle of existence but were also to replace our sense of self-importance with a profound sense of the importance of others, the peace that we would attain would be one characterized by a dynamic responsiveness to the suffering of others, replete with wisdom, compassion, and power. This is the fully complete enlightenment of a buddha, attained by virtue of Mahāyāna practices.

How do we eliminate our self-centeredness and the mistaken sense of self that underlies it? By cultivating relative and absolute enlightened attitudes, respectively. Formal meditation alone is not enough to produce the radical transformation that will entirely eliminate our self-centeredness and the sense of self that underlies it. Those attitudes run deep. They are innate perspectives that we have become habituated to in life after life since time immemorial. Our sense of self affects every choice we make, everything we do or don't do. It may seem that we secure our happiness and safety by looking out for ourselves first of all, but the Buddha taught that this type of attitude is really the source of our unhappiness, for under the sway of self-centeredness we act at the expense of others. Our selfish actions lead to reincarnation in lives filled with hardship and difficult experiences, wherein our selfish way of thinking is further reinforced, leading to further experiences of misery, and so on and on.

In order to overcome the deeply rooted self-centeredness and the basic sense of self that underlies it, our meditation must go hand in hand with a dedicated effort to bring the practice of training the mind into our daily lives—into every moment, every situation, with everyone we meet. In short, training the mind is a 24/7, around-the-clock practice, or it should be as close to that as possible. Training the mind involves never straying from implementation of the methods for developing the two types of enlightened attitude in order to remedy the two types of self-involvement. Conceived of in this way, when training the mind, our practice of meditation and our behavior throughout the rest of our day come to complement and enhance one another.

When we bring the practice of training our minds into our everyday lives, experiences of adversity become opportunities to deepen our practice. Simply carrying the precepts of training our minds into the world as we go about our business produces a dramatic shift in our ordinary perspective. Rather than reacting to unpleasant experiences with aversion, annoyance, and withdrawal, we come to enthusiastically embrace them, grateful for the opportunity to practice transforming our self-importance into a sense of the importance of others. What could be a more radical transformation of our perspective than being able to feel sincere gratitude to others for causing us problems? What could be more different from our usual mindset than seeing sickness, aging, and even death as profound opportunities? Contrary to what one would expect, learning to see the difficulties and challenges in our lives as opportunities to transform our hearts and minds actually produces a very robust and stable sense of happiness and well-being that endures, come what may. This, in fact, is "the promise" of mind training.

A lifetime's practice of training the mind can be summarized in five powers: the powers of resolve, familiarity, the positive seed, eradication, and prayer. These five, which summarize the mindset of continuous training, are said to be the essence of Mahāyāna instructions. They serve to develop and reinforce the enlightened attitude both during our lives and at the moment of death. The five powers provide clear guidelines as to what our priority should be: to work constantly at eradicating our self-centered attitude and basic mistaken sense of self.

How do we measure the success of our training? We know that our training has been effective when our familiarity with the practices is such that we no longer regress in them and are able to keep them up even when distracted. In other words, we are trained when we spontaneously and naturally react to whatever happens with a profound sense of the importance of others.

The commitments and precepts for training the mind summarize the things we must do and what we must stop doing in order for the training to be successful. Observance of the commitments and adherence to the precepts provides the discipline needed to make real headway against the innate sense that we are special and more important than others. Without this sort of discipline, we are likely to continually slip back into our habitual mode of selfishness, even if only in subtle ways. In this sense, the commitments and precepts make us more vigilant and self-aware as we work to change ourselves for the better.

Once we have taken up the practice of training the mind, we should carry it on no matter what type of challenges life may throw at us, even if that challenge is our own inevitable death. Of course, as beginners it is difficult to imagine being able to handle a challenge as overwhelming as death, but if we practice steadily and consistently, over time we will come to even look at death as an opportunity to transform ourselves. The more that we let go of our self-centeredness and the basic mistaken sense of self that underlies it, and the more we come to understand the value of others as a consequence of having let go, the easier and more happy life becomes. A well-known verse of *In Reverence to the Guru* says:

> Holding myself dear is the cause of all my suffering;
> Holding others dear is the basis of all that is
>   wonderful.[9]

Training our minds in the way outlined by Chekawa in his *Seven-Point Mind Training* and elaborated upon by Gomo Tulku in his *Annotations to Foundational Verses for Training the Mind* will enable us to overcome self-centeredness and lead fully compassionate lives. The goal of this practice is a state of perfect mental and spiritual health—the enlightenment of a buddha. Training our minds is therefore the best medicine, the best therapy, and the best psychology. The benefits for ourselves and others can be immense. It is up to us to put the practice of training the mind to the test.

Joan Nicell
Kopan Monastery
Kathmandu, Nepal
March 2014

FOUNDATIONAL VERSES OF SEVEN-POINT MIND TRAINING

BY CHEKAWA YESHÉ DORJÉ

Homage to great compassion.

These instructions, the essence of nectar,
are the lineage from Serlingpa.
They are like a diamond, the sun, and a medicinal tree.
Understand the point and so forth of these texts.
Transform the worsening fivefold degeneration into the path
   to enlightenment.

I. FOUNDATIONAL PRACTICES TO BUILD YOUR CAPACITY

First, train in the preliminaries.

II. TRAINING THE MIND IN THE PATH TO ENLIGHTENMENT

Put all the blame on one.
Meditate on everyone as very kind.
Train alternately in taking and giving.

Begin the sequence of taking with yourself.

Mount the two astride the breath.

There are three objects, three poisons, and three roots of
virtue.

These are the condensed instructions for the post-meditation
period.

Be mindful of them in order to admonish yourself.

Train with the words in all activities.

Having achieved stability, learn the secret.

Regard phenomena as dreamlike.

Examine the nature of unborn awareness.

The antidote itself is also free right where it is.

Focus on the nature of the basis of all, the entity of the path.

Between sessions be an illusionist.

III. Using Adversity on the Path to Enlightenment

When the container and its contents are filled with negativity,
transform adverse conditions into the path to enlightenment.
Immediately apply whatever you encounter to meditation.
To possess the four practices is the best of methods.

IV. A Lifetime's Practice Summarized

The summarized essence of the instructions is:
apply yourself to the five powers.
The Mahāyāna instructions for transferring consciousness
are precisely these five powers; cherish this conduct.

V. The Measure of a Trained Mind

Gather all Dharmas into one intent.
Of the two witnesses uphold the main one.
Always rely on a happy mind alone.
The measure of being trained is to no longer regress.
The sign of being trained is to be great in five ways.
If this can be done even when distracted, you are trained.

VI. The Commitments of Mind Training

Constantly train in three general points.
Change your attitude while remaining as you are.
Don't speak of others' defects.
Don't reflect on others' shortcomings.
First purify whatever affliction is strongest.
Give up all hope of reward.
Discard poisoned food.
Don't hold a grudge.
Don't mock with malicious sarcasm.
Don't lie in ambush.
Don't strike at the heart.
Don't put a horse's load on a pony.
Don't sprint to win a race.
Don't misuse this practice as a rite.
Don't turn a god into a demon.
Don't seek suffering as a means to happiness.

VII. The Precepts of Mind Training

Do all yogas single-mindedly.
Overcome all misguiding influences with one.
There are two acts: one at the beginning and one at the end.
Bear whichever of the two arises.
Guard two at the cost of your life.
Train in three difficulties.
Adopt three principal causes.
Cultivate three without allowing them to deteriorate.
Possess three inseparably.
Train in purity and impartiality with respect to objects.
Train inclusively and profoundly: cherish all.
Ever acquaint yourself with special cases.
Don't depend on other conditions.
Take up what is most important right now.
Avoid understanding wrongly.
Don't be sporadic.
Train with decisiveness.
Free yourself with the duo of investigation and analysis.
Don't boast.
Don't be bad tempered.
Don't be fickle.
Don't wish for gratitude.

Colophon

Disregarding suffering and slander
I sought out instruction in taming selfishness
because of my many aspirations.
Now I have no regrets even when I die.

A PROLOGUE
TO TRAINING THE MIND

Namo guruye!

I bow to the Kinsman of the Sun who revealed the instructions for training in bodhicitta—the quintessence of the 84,000 collections of Dharma that he, the Peerless Teacher and Lord of the Ten Powers, taught.

I BEGIN MY COMMENTARY on the *Foundational Verses for Training the Mind*[10] by paying homage or bowing to the holy being, Śākyamuni Buddha, for whom Kinsman of the Sun, Peerless Teacher, and Lord of the Ten Powers are poetic epithets. Bodhicitta—the altruistic aspiration to attain enlightenment for the benefit of all sentient beings—is the very essence of the 84,000 collections of teachings that he taught as antidotes to the 84,000 afflictions.

With heartfelt reverence, I bow with body, speech, and mind to the actual and lineage holy beings, Serlingpa, Dīpaṃkara, and the rest, who came one after the other—the source of these precious instructions on training the mind as taught by the Kinsman of the Sun.

Next I pay homage to my actual gurus and to the lineage gurus who were responsible for transmitting the instructions for developing bodhicitta. These instructions were passed down from Dharmakīrti of Sumatra, known as Serlingpa (the Sumantran) in Tibetan, to his Indian disciple Dīpaṃkara Śrījñāna (982–1054), better known as Atiśa. Atiśa, in turn, passed them to his foremost Tibetan disciple, Dromtönpa (1005–64), who then passed them to the Kadam geshe, Potowa (1031–1106). Geshe Potowa transmitted them to his disciple Geshe Sharawa (1070–1141), who subsequently passed them on to Geshe Chekawa (1101–75). It is this master who is renowned for having put the mind training teachings into practice, and for having encapsulated them in seven points with his text *Seven-Point Mind Training*. He did this to simplify the mind training teachings and to make it easier for others to practice them. Geshe Chekawa originally wrote his text in prose form. It was only later, in the early nineteenth century, that Keutsang Jamyang Mönlam Rinpoche rendered the work into verse, titling the resultant text *Foundational Verses for Training the Mind*.

The mind training teachings were transmitted in an unbroken lineage from Geshe Chekawa to Pabongkha Rinpoche, from whom I received the oral transmission. The mere fact that these teachings have been transmitted in an unbroken lineage from teacher to disciple makes them of great benefit to a practitioner's mind. However, this is not the only reason they are of benefit: they were also learned, put into practice, and realized by the gurus of the past.

Having expressed my homage, I will now discuss
Foundational Verses for Training the Mind.

There are a great variety of mind training texts, some being very detailed and extensive, while others are very concise. However, they all share the same purpose: they were written to show how to train one's mind in order to attain enlightenment for the benefit of all sentient beings.

Homage to great compassion.

This line expresses homage to great loving compassion, the main topic of this text.

Geshe Chekawa, author of *Seven-Point Mind Training*, pays homage to the actual topic of his text—the great compassion present in the minds of all buddhas.

THE ESSENCE OF THE BUDDHA'S TEACHINGS

These instructions, the essence of nectar, ...

The Buddha's teachings destroy without exception the suffering of birth, aging, sickness, death, and so on, produced by the 84,000 afflictions. In addition, they easily grant nonabiding nirvana." These instructions are the essence, or nectar, of His teachings. In other words, they are the quintessence of the 84,000 collections of Dharma.

As mentioned above, the Buddha taught 84,000 collections of Dharma as antidotes to the 84,000 afflictions. These afflictions are responsible for producing every type of suffering, including our human sufferings of birth, aging, sickness, and death. Bodhicitta, the enlightened attitude, is the actual antidote that destroys these 84,000 afflictions. If the 84,000 teachings were condensed, we would find their very essence to be the mind training practices, which we engage in for the specific purpose of developing bodhicitta.

Bodhicitta is the principal cause for achieving the state of buddhahood, whereas realization of emptiness[12] is the principal cause for achieving liberation from cyclic existence. Realization of emptiness—wisdom[13]—without bodhicitta—method[14]—is said to be bondage, while realization of emptiness conjoined with bodhicitta is said to bring freedom. This is so because if one's realization of emptiness is not sustained by bodhicitta, one will only achieve the personal peace of nirvana. Although *śrāvaka* and *pratyekabuddha arhats*[15] attain direct realizations of emptiness and the state of nirvana, because they lack great compassion they are unable to achieve the state of enlightenment. Because they neglect all other suffering sentient beings, their nirvana is considered to be a type of bondage. Likewise, if one possesses bodhicitta but lacks any realization of emptiness, this too would be bondage because one would remain bound in the prison of cyclic existence by one's mental afflictions. When realization of emptiness is sustained by great compassion, it results in great liberation, the state of buddhahood. Therefore, to achieve the state of perfectly complete enlightenment it is essential to unify the practices of method and wisdom.

The Mind Training Lineage

... are the lineage from Serlingpa.

These instructions belong to Guru Serlingpa, but combine the lineages of Guru Dharmarakṣita, Guru Maitri-yogi, and Guru Serlingpa into one stream. Moreover, they constitute the tradition of Kadam geshe Chekawa's *Seven-Point Mind Training*.

The Indian masters Atiśa (982–1054) and Śāntideva (c. 700) are the sources of two well-known techniques of mind training used to develop bodhicitta. The mind training practice that comes down to us from Atiśa is commonly known as "sevenfold cause and effect," while that which comes down to us from Śāntideva is known as "equalizing and exchanging oneself with others."

Three principal gurus transmitted mind training teaching lineages to Atiśa: Dharmarakṣita, Maitriyogi, and Serlingpa. The particular mind training instructions summarized in *Seven-Point Mind Training* originate with Serlingpa. Atiśa had heard that it was possible to receive instructions on how to develop bodhicitta from this master, and he set off on a long and dangerous sea voyage to Sumatra. The journey took many months and, among the numerous difficulties encountered, a huge storm threatened to destroy the ship en route. Twenty-one emanations of the goddess Tārā appeared and protected the ship from harm as a result of Atiśa's fervent prayers for help.

After arriving safely Atiśa received the instructions for developing bodhicitta from Serlingpa. Because these instructions are the means to attain enlightenment, Atiśa always considered Serlingpa to be his most important guru, despite having many others.

Years later Atiśa was invited to Tibet where he devoted the latter part of his life to the propagation and preservation of Buddhism in that country. There he transmitted the instructions on bodhicitta to his foremost disciple, Dromtönpa, from whom they have been passed down in an unbroken lineage to our present-day teachers.

Similes for Mind Training Instructions

They are like a diamond, the sun, and a medicinal tree.

Just as, even when broken, a precious diamond still outshines all the finest jewelry, likewise, those who possess merely a fraction of the instructions on the precious bodhicitta outshine all śrāvaka and pratyeka-buddha arhats. Just as, even when the sun is still rising, its rays dispel the darkness of night, likewise, the mere possession of the instructions for training in bodhicitta dispels the darkness of selfishness, deluded ignorance. And just as even the branches and leaves of a medicinal tree are able to alleviate the 404 diseases,[16] likewise, even a fraction of the instructions for training in bodhicitta is able to alleviate the chronic disease of the 84,000 afflictions.

The usefulness and value of the instructions for training in the enlightened attitude of bodhicitta are demonstrated by way of three similes that compare them to a diamond, the sun, and a medicinal tree.

Just as even a tiny fragment of a diamond outshines all other precious jewels, likewise, those who possess even a tiny portion of instruction in relative bodhicitta outshine all others, even the śrāvakas and pratyekabuddhas. Just as even when still rising the sun naturally dispels darkness, likewise, even possessing the instructions for training in absolute bodhicitta naturally dispels the darkness of ignorance. Just as even a part of a medicinal tree is able to cure disease, likewise, even a part of the instructions for training in bodhicitta is able to eliminate the disease afflicting our minds—the 84,000 afflictions.

The Point of the Mind Training Texts

Understand the point and so forth of these texts.[17]

The main point, or topic, of these texts is the instructions for training in bodhicitta.

The point of all mindtraining texts is to instruct one in the development of relative and absolute bodhicitta. Geshe Chekawa mentions this to emphasize the fact that the main point of the many texts on mind training is the same:

to explain the practices for training in the two enlightened attitudes.

Transforming Adverse Conditions into the Path

Transform the worsening fivefold degeneration into the path to enlightenment.

The fivefold degeneration relates to time, sentient beings, affliction, life span, and views. Degeneration of these five is presently worsening, such that there are few conditions for happiness, much harm from humans and nonhumans, and many occasions for contending with negative circumstances. It is at times like this that we should transform such adverse conditions into the path to enlightenment.

Because we live in a period in which the fivefold degeneration is worsening, we are forced to experience many types of adverse conditions, caused by humans and other types of beings. At the same time, good conditions grow increasingly rare, with the result that we regularly run into problems when we try to do something positive and tend to meet with little success. It is very important, for these reasons, that we use the practices of mind training to transform all such adverse conditions into the path to enlightenment.

1: FOUNDATIONAL PRACTICES TO BUILD YOUR CAPACITY

First, train in the preliminaries.

Train your mind in the stages of the path for those who have a lesser motivation by reflecting on: the great meaning of this life of freedom and opportunity, the difficulty of obtaining it, death and impermanence, the fact that nothing other than Dharma will be of benefit at the time of death, the sufferings of the three lower realms, taking refuge, and actions and their consequences.

Then, train your mind well in the stages of the path for those who have a middling motivation by reflecting on: suffering, beginning with the drawbacks of cyclic existence (i.e., there is no certainty with respect to friends and enemies, there is no satisfaction here, the body must be repeatedly lost, we must be repeatedly reborn, our station continually changes, we must be parted from friends and relatives), the suffering generally associated with cyclic existence (i.e., suffering because things change, suffering pain and misery, and the pervasive suffering that we continuously compound), and the suffering of the higher realms in particular (i.e., birth, aging, sickness, and death for human beings, death after a long and happy life for the gods, and jealous rivalry for the demigods).

THE PRELIMINARY PRACTICES consist of the various meditations intended for people of lesser and middling motivations or capabilities. They form the foundation of the principal practice for those of great capability—training in bodhicitta. As practitioners of mind training we should first familiarize ourselves with these meditations before engaging in the actual practice of training the mind.

The practices for those who have a lesser motivation, or people of lesser capability, include meditating on such topics as devotion to the guru, the great meaning of this precious human life possessed of freedom and opportunity, death and impermanence, and so on. Having gained facility in these meditations, practitioners should subsequently take up the practices for those who have middling motivations, or people of middling capability, meditating on such topics as the drawbacks of cyclic existence, the suffering of cyclic existence in general, the suffering particular to the higher realms, and so on.

PRACTICES FOR
PEOPLE OF LESSER CAPABILITY

Those who have a lesser motivation, or people of lesser capability, are so called because their motivation for pursuing spiritual practice is only to achieve happiness for themselves in future lives by avoiding rebirth into any of the three lower realms. Practitioners of lesser capability meditate on six main topics: devotion to the guru, the meaningfulness and difficulty of obtaining a precious human life, death and impermanence, suffering associated with the lower realms, taking refuge, and actions and their consequences.

Devotion to the guru

In general, there are two types of religious people: the first rush to listen to a well-known teacher as soon as they hear that the teacher is scheduled to teach without first examining that teacher's qualities, but the second take the time to investigate the qualities of a particular teacher, try to determine whether that teacher actually practices what they preach, and only place their faith in a teacher or take them as a guru after having determined that the teacher is well qualified. The first type of person, who is less intelligent, can be called "a person who follows based on faith." The second type of person, who is more intelligent, can be called "a person who follows based on reason." When the kind of preliminary examination used by people who follow based on reason is done, a disciple's devotion to the guru will be stable and they will run no risk of it deteriorating.

If, after examining a particular teacher, we find them to be qualified, we should heed the advice of an old Tibetan saying and "act like a blind man holding the tail of a cow." Once a blind person has caught hold of a cow's tail in order to follow the course of a path, he dare not risk letting go. If, on the other hand, he holds tightly and resolutely to the cow's tail, he will safely reach his destination. Likewise, to achieve success in our spiritual practice, it is crucial that we remain very stable and consistent in our devotion to our guru; we should not change gurus for any reason. If we behave in this way, we can definitely attain realization, even within the very short lifetime characteristic of this degenerate age.

The cultivation of devotion to the guru is divided into four points: devotion to the guru in thought, devotion to the guru in action, reflecting on the advantages of being properly devoted to the guru, and reflecting on the disadvantages of being improperly devoted to the guru.

Devotion to the guru in thought

The kindness of my gurus—from my very first guru who taught me the alphabet up to my last guru who taught me the most profound teachings—is the main reason for my having been able to bring about a change in my mind, to be consistent in the practice of training my mind, and to develop positive states of mind. In short, any beneficial result that I have experienced from the practice of training my mind is mainly due to the blessings I received from my gurus.

An anecdote from the life of the Indian master Atiśa, who spent the last seventeen years of his life teaching in Tibet, is often recounted to demonstrate the importance of devotion to the guru. Atiśa was once asked why none of the many meditators in Tibet had gained any spiritual realization. Atiśa responded that it was because Tibetans tended to think of their gurus as ordinary people. I too have met many people over the years that have told me that they had yet to gain any realization, despite having practiced Dharma for quite some time. My own opinion is that this is due to a lack of devotion to their guru.

We can turn to reliable scripture to develop devotion to the guru, the essence of which is to see the guru as a buddha in actuality. In a frequently cited passage from a tantra, for example, Vajradhara explicitly states that the guru is in reality a buddha. This statement is considered to be reliable because the spiritual victor Vajradhara founded the whole tantric path. As such, this citation is considered sufficient evidence for establishing that the guru is indeed a buddha; one need not present any other evidence. However, to further develop our conviction that the guru is in fact a buddha, we may also turn to quotations from such reliable scriptures as Maitreya's *Ornament for Clear Realization* (*Abhisamayālaṃkāra*). In the eighth chapter of this particular text there are several verses that have personally inspired me very much and helped strengthen my faith that the guru is an actual manifestation of a buddha. Two such verses are:

> The miraculous body[18] of the sage is that which
>   impartially enacts
> manifold benefit for the world, unabated for as
>   long it endures.[19]

And:

> So it is said that its work continues unabated as
>   long as samsara lasts.[20]

What Maitreya is saying with these verses is that in the future buddhas will appear in a variety of ways to guide beings of diverse standing and capability. Buddhas use this approach because spiritually unevolved people would be unable to perceive them if they were to appear directly in their actual form as buddhas. As Pabongkha Rinpoche tells us in *Liberation in the Palm of Your Hand*, we are very fortunate, in spite of our mental obscuration, that we are even able to see our guru in human form and not, for example, as an animal. In other words, if we bore any more karmic obscuration, we wouldn't even be able to see our guru as a human but would instead perceive him as a horse, a dog, or perhaps a donkey!

To illustrate how fortunate we are in this regard, we can recall an event that happened not long ago concerning a certain Kagyu lama named Losang Tönden:

> One day when Losang Tönden was teaching near Drepung Monastery, among the thousands of people listening to him was a monk who was unable to see or hear him teaching. This monk instead perceived the lama to be sitting on the throne eating meat.

This story illustrates how people can perceive the same guru in different ways according to their particular karmic obscuration. To avoid having such distorted perceptions in the future, it is important to practice seeing the guru's every act as wholesome and meaningful and to pray that we are always able to see the guru in human form.

By thinking about the qualities and kindness of our gurus we develop deep faith in and respect for them, as a consequence of which we properly devote ourselves to them in thought.

Devotion to the guru in action

Devotion to the guru in action involves doing physical acts, such as serving our gurus by helping them in whatever way is needed, offering them things, and generally engaging in actions that please them. In my own case, all my gurus were extremely good and kind to me, and I always tried to practice very pure devotion toward them. I would express my devotion to them, for example, by taking exceptional care of their belongings, never gossiping about other people with them, and avoiding even stepping on their shadows.

The advantages of being properly devoted to the guru

One of the benefits of devotion to the guru is that we will be able to quickly understand whatever they teach and apply it directly in our spiritual practice because we have pure faith in them as a teacher. By being purely devoted to the guru we will eventually be able to serve as many as a thousand gurus without any flaw in our devotion. Without pure devotion to the guru, even if we hear teachings from a very highly qualified lama they will be of little benefit to our minds.

In short, the advantages of being properly devoted to the guru in thought and action are that we will please our guru and that the buddhas will consequently respond by blessing us through the guru.

The disadvantages of being improperly devoted to the guru
Once the Buddha was asked about the disadvantages of being improperly devoted to the guru. Although he replied at great length, the gist of his response was that the consequence of being improperly devoted to the guru is bad rebirth. This particular result is discussed in a passage from *Liberation in the Palm of Your Hand*, where it says that as a result of improper devotion to the guru one will be reborn a hundred times as a dog and then as a human being of low class. In light of these and other disadvantages, we should take great care not to act improperly in terms of devotion to the guru.

In sum, given that success in training the mind depends on having a firm foundation of pure devotion to the guru, I want to emphasize how necessary it is to do this right from the very beginning of your spiritual practice. However, although this is my advice, I am merely presenting this topic to you; it is up to you to make your own decision as to whether or not you wish to be devoted to a guru.

Lastly, although disciples definitely must have sincere devotion to the guru, the guru should not have any expectations of his disciples. Lama Tsongkhapa warns us about this in his teachings on the stages of the path, where he notes that a guru being extremely unhappy when disciples make small mistakes and being excessively pleased when they make him an offering is a sign that the guru is not qualified to lead them on the path to enlightenment.[21]

Precious human life

Once we have cultivated devotion to the guru for some time, we should begin to reflect on the value of our precious human life and how difficult it is to obtain such a life again. Our precious human lives are characterized by eightfold freedom and ten points of opportunity. The eightfold freedom of this life is being free from the life of hell beings, free from the life of animals, free from the life of hungry ghosts, free from the life of long-lived gods, free from life in barbaric countries, free from a life of mental or sensory impairment such as being deaf and dumb, free from holding wrong views, and free from living at a time when a buddha has not taught.

Were we to be born into a situation that lacks any of these freedoms, we would not have the opportunity to practice Dharma. So it is said that only those of us who have these freedoms—and therefore the conditions necessary to be able to practice Dharma—have a "precious" human life. Thus, a precious human life should not be confused with just any human life. An anecdote about an exchange that happened once in Tibet perfectly captures this type of misunderstanding:

> One day a well-known lama, Purchog Ngawang Jampa, was teaching about the precious human life, its freedom and opportunity, and the difficulty of getting such a life. Among the many people listening to his teaching there was a Chinese man who raised an objection on this point. He spoke up, saying, "Surely you have never visited China. If you

had, you would certainly have seen the enormous numbers of Chinese people and understood that a human life is not so difficult to obtain at all!"

In addition to eightfold freedom, our precious human lives also have ten points of opportunity. These ten can be subdivided into five points of personal opportunity and five points of circumstantial opportunity. The five points of personal opportunity come from having been born as a human being, having been born in a central country where Dharma exists, being mentally and physically unimpaired, being unburdened by commission of any of the five acts that bring immediate retribution, and having faith in the Three Jewels. The five points of circumstantial opportunity come from the facts that a buddha has come to this world, has turned the wheel of Dharma, his teachings still exist, as do ordained people and those who have love and compassion for people who practice Dharma.

It is essential that we take advantage of our great fortune at having obtained a precious human life. If we fail to do so, this rare opportunity will have been squandered: we would end up like someone who sets out to find precious jewels, arrives at a place filled with them, and then returns empty-handed. A tale recounted in *Essential Nectar* illustrates how important it is to take advantage of this precious human life:

Once upon a time there was an blind old man. One day, while walking on a hillside, he fell over a ledge and landed on the back of a wild ass. The ass, who had never before allowed anyone to ride him, began to run very fast. The old man held very tightly to the ass's mane, but the tighter he held, the faster the ass ran. Eventually, they burst into a busy marketplace. Many people saw the blind old man clinging to the ass and wondered what had happened. The blind man pretended that he was purposely sitting on the ass and began to sing. When asked what he was doing, he replied, "If I don't sing today, when should I?"[22]

So, like a blind old man enjoying the rare opportunity of riding a wild ass, we should make use of this perfect human life—so rare and precious—in a meaningful way, while we still have the chance. This is an extremely important piece of advice.

Death and impermanence

Although we have this precious human life now, we are completely uncertain about when we will die, and the human life span is generally highly variable. Buddhist scriptures indicate how variable human life spans have been, saying that although human beings once had a life span of 80,000 years, it gradually decreased to its present length of about a hundred years, maximum. Regarding our uncertainty about when death will actually come, the stages of the path teachings[23] remind us that we cannot know which will happen first: tomorrow morning or the next life. These teachings emphasize the uncertainty of our lives in order to urge us to put the Dharma into practice right now.

By reflecting on the fragility of this precious human life, the fact that death will certainly happen to all of us, and that our only aid at the time of death will be our prior practice of Dharma, we develop a strong determination to practice Dharma right now. Having practiced Dharma throughout our lives, we will be able to die without fear and secure a good rebirth. However, if we don't practice Dharma in our lives, we will be depressed and afraid when we die and be born into lower realms, where we will experience much suffering.

The suffering associated with the lower realms

Next, to further motivate ourselves to engage in spiritual practice without delay, we should reflect on the suffering experienced by beings in the three lower realms—denizens of hell, hungry ghosts, and animals. In the context of thinking of the suffering of these beings, we reflect on how beings born in the two main realms of hell suffer extreme heat and cold, how beings born as hungry ghosts suffer hunger and thirst, and how beings born as animals on land, in the sea, and scattered throughout the domains of gods and humans suffer being crowded together in countless numbers and being eaten by each other or enslaved by humans.

Taking refuge

Then, to safeguard ourselves against low rebirth, reflect on the qualities of the Three Jewels—the Buddha, Dharma, and Sangha—and seek refuge in them from the depths of your hearts.

Actions and their consequences

Whether turning to the Three Jewels for refuge will be much help to us or not depends entirely on our behavior. Our own negative acts are what lead us to the lower realms, so in addition to taking refuge in the Three Jewels, we must also be extremely careful not to commit even the slightest negative act. If, however, we do mistakenly commit a nonvirtuous act, even a small one, we should not ignore it. Instead we should immediately confess it because the strength of an act naturally increases over time. If, for example, we were to kill an insect today and not confess it, the negative act would continue to increase in strength day by day. To train one's mind it is absolutely essential to have a good understanding of the law of actions and their consequences or *karma*—unwholesome acts bring suffering and wholesome acts bring happiness. This is so because ethical discipline is the very basis on which to train one's mind.

Practices for People of Middling Capability

When we have come to hold a middling motivation, or become people of middling capability, we are not just motivated by the desire to avoid rebirth in the three lower realms, we also seek to gain liberation from the cycle of existence altogether. Yet although this attitude is superior to that of people of lesser capability, it is still inferior to the attitude of those who have the greatest motivation. People of great capability wish not only to eliminate what causes

suffering in their own minds—the mental afflictions—
they also strive to attain enlightenment in order to help
all other sentient beings gain their own freedom from the
cycle of existence.

To become people of middling capability we must
reflect on the varieties of suffering experienced throughout
existence, summarized as the six drawbacks[24] and threefold
suffering[25] general to existence. We must do so to gain a
deep and clear understanding that even life in the three
higher realms—whether god, demigod, or human—is still
by nature suffering. We must also reflect on the suffering
that uniquely characterizes each of these realms. Human
beings, for example, experience eight types of suffering in
particular: they are born, they fall sick, they age, they die,
they are deprived of what they find pleasant, they encounter what they find unpleasant, they do not find what they
seek, and finally, they have bodies which suffer by their very
nature.

Gods experience three types of suffering in particular:
they live an incredibly long time, they experience signs of
their impending deaths, and they know that they must
once again fall into the lower realms. The suffering peculiar
to demigods is that, due to their intense jealousy, they continually, yet always unsuccessfully, go to war with the gods.

In short, even if we were born into one of the higher
realms as a human, demigod, or god, we would unavoid-
ably experience the suffering general to existence, as well as
the suffering specific to whatever realm we would be born
into.

2: TRAINING THE MIND IN THE PATH TO ENLIGHTENMENT

A Relative Enlightened Attitude

Put all the blame on one.

Other than our own mistaken sense of self and self-importance, there is no one else whosoever, human or otherwise, whom we can blame for our unhappiness. The self-importance induced by the deluded ignorance in our minds leads us to ignore the distinction between virtue and nonvirtue and causes us to be jealous of our superiors, to scorn our inferiors, and to compete with our peers. When we understand that the sole instigator of our misery throughout cyclic existence without beginning, even to this moment, has been precisely this attitude, we will enter the community of people who practice Dharma. Therefore, we must blame our sense of self-importance.

We should put the blame for all our problems on one source alone: our self-centered, self-important attitude.

Our sense of self-importance is to blame because it leads us to ignore the law of actions and their consequences, whereby we engage in negative acts that bring the result of miserable rebirth and unpleasant experiences.

In our everyday lives, when we end up in a difficult situation we tend to rationalize by thinking, "It wasn't I who caused this problem." We point our fingers at others and say, "They are to blame." We should stop thinking in this way when we take up the practice of training our minds. Instead, we should try to understand that every unpleasant experience comes from the selfish attitude of cherishing ourselves more than others. We should keep in mind that it is not some higher being who sends us to be born in the various types of unpleasant life as a punishment, but that those lives and the suffering they entail are caused by our own selfish minds.

The mental state of ignorance is the basic error that underlies all of our unpleasant experiences. Ignorance serves as the basis for the self-important attitude that leads us to act wrongly, to be jealous of people who are superior to us, to be arrogant and haughty toward people whom we consider inferior, and to compete with those who are our equals. In short, we must clearly understand that all the various problems and suffering we experience are caused by our own self-important minds. For this reason the Kadam geshes used to call the self-important mind "the owl-headed augur of bad omens."[26] In the end, whether or not we are good Buddhists is determined by the degree to which we cherish ourselves above others.

Meditate on everyone as very kind.

Every happiness and virtue in our minds come about through other sentient beings. Therefore, we must reflect in general on the great kindness of sentient beings, our former mothers, and must particularly reflect on the great kindness of harmful beings, human or otherwise.

Whenever you experience undesired pain—even something as minor as the bite of a fly or an ant—think, "From time without beginning I have eaten this being's flesh and drunk its blood. This bite is payment for that karmic debt," thus letting go of any harmful intent toward those who have done you harm. Then, since the time has come to repay the debt, pray that the karmic debt be purified, thus transforming undesired harm into an aid for developing the precious enlightened attitude— bodhicitta. Apply methods or at the very least fervently pray that even those living beings that have harmed us develop precious bodhicitta in their hearts and minds.

For Langri Thangpa said, "The essential point of the many profound Dharma texts that I have opened and examined is that all mistakes are our own, while all good qualities belong to noble sentient beings. So give the profit and victory to others and take the loss and defeat upon yourself." He also said that there is nothing to understand other than this.

Whatever happiness we experience comes about either directly or indirectly because of the kindness of other sentient beings. Even those who harm us are actually very helpful and kind because they provide us with an opportunity to develop an enlightened attitude. For these reasons, we must reflect on all sentient beings, without exception, as being very kind to us.

Whenever we experience mental or physical problems, whether big or small, we should reflect that they are the result of our own past actions. We shouldn't get angry even when a fly or an ant bites us and think to kill it. We should reflect instead that the reason that we suffer being bitten is that at some time in the past we drank its blood and ate its flesh. Thinking in this way we can feel glad that we now have the opportunity to repay a debt created in previous lives. Likewise, if a person threatens or beats us, or some spirit makes us sick, rather than develop hatred for them it would be much better to transform such adverse conditions into means for developing an enlightened attitude. To do so we should reflect, as Langri Thangpa says, that all our positive qualities come from other living beings, while all of our negativities come from our own side. Thus it is right to give the victory to others and to take the defeat on ourselves. We can also pray, "May all those who harm me quickly develop an enlightened attitude."

Train alternately in taking and giving.

Train alternately in taking and giving[27] by equalizing and exchanging yourself and others. Imagine yourself as able to give your happiness and virtue to other sentient beings and able to take the negativities and sufferings of other sentient beings onto yourself. As *Rays of Sunlight Mind Training* says, "Presently, aside from merely contemplating taking and giving, it is difficult to actually take the wrongs and suffering of others upon ourselves. But when you have trained and familiarized yourself with this practice, it will not be difficult to actually take them. Therefore, train your mind."

We must train in the contemplation of taking and giving, wherein we take on ourselves all the wrongs, suffering, and so on, of other beings and give them all our happiness, roots of virtue, and so on. In connection with the practice of taking and giving, *Rays of Sunlight Mind Training* says that although it might be difficult to train in taking and giving at the beginning, eventually, through training ourselves well, we will be able to actually take upon ourselves the suffering of others.

Begin the sequence of taking with yourself.

When your wish to take others' sufferings upon yourself is weak, first develop courage by skillfully training as follows: in the morning take upon yourself the suffering you will experience in the afternoon; then take upon yourself now the suffering you will experience next year, in future lives, and so on.

If we are unable to take even our own problems upon ourselves, we will obviously be unable to take on the suffering of others. So when we practice taking we should begin by taking on our own future suffering. We can begin by taking on right now, at this moment, the problems that we will experience later on today and tomorrow. Next we can gradually take on this week the problems that we will experience next week. Then we can take on this year the problems that we will experience next year, and so on. We continue in this way until we are able to take upon ourselves in this very life even the problems we will encounter in future lives. By training gradually like this, eventually we will also be able to take the suffering of others upon ourselves.

Mount the two astride the breath.

During the post-meditation period, give all your roots of virtue of the three times to all sentient beings, your former mothers, as you exhale through your right nostril. Imagine that they all thereby attain uncontaminated happiness. Then, while inhaling through your left nostril, take upon yourself all the wrongs and suffering of all your mother sentient beings of old, and imagine that they are all freed from suffering.

"The two," taking and giving, are to be practiced in conjunction with inhalation and exhalation. As you breathe out through your right nostril, visualize giving your happiness, wealth, and roots of virtue of the three times (past, present, and future) to all sentient beings in the form of white light. While breathing in through your left nostril, visualize taking upon yourself all their negative deeds, suffering, and so on in the form of black smoke. In addition, think that all the suffering that other beings are to experience in the future is experienced by you right now, completely freeing them even from suffering in the future.

There are three objects, three poisons, and three roots of virtue.

The three objects are enemies, friends, and strangers; the three poisons are attachment, hatred, and delusion; and the three roots of virtue are any virtuous practices unmixed with attachment, hatred, and delusion.

The three objects are the three types of people—namely those we categorize as friends, enemies, and strangers. The three poisons are attachment, hatred, and delusion, which arise in relation to the three objects, respectively. In other words, we are attached to our friends, hate our enemies, and are indifferent to strangers. The three roots of virtue are virtuous practices that are not mixed with attachment, hatred, or delusion. This implies that for an action to be virtuous, including dedicating merit to the achievement of enlightenment, our minds must be free from the three mental poisons.

These are the condensed instructions for the post-meditation period.

The condensed instructions are to exchange your position with that of others by giving away your own virtues to sentient beings and taking their suffering upon yourself.

All instructions can be boiled down to the mind training practice of giving our happiness to others and taking their suffering upon ourselves.

Be mindful of them in order to admonish yourself.

Admonish yourself by being ever mindful of whether your heart transgresses the Mahāyāna practice of training the mind.

We need to be constantly mindful of whether we violate or maintain the Mahāyāna practice of training the mind. Then if we catch ourselves doing something that contradicts our practice we will be able to immediately quit doing it. This is why we should be sure to maintain a mental state of mindfulness during all our activities.

Train with the words in all activities.

Never, during any activity whatsoever, including walking, standing, lying, and sitting, allow your heart to be parted from the work of training the mind. Recite words from mind training texts to aid in this.

We must continuously train ourselves in virtue by not allowing our minds to be parted from the work of training the mind. We can prevent this from happening by reciting the words of mind training texts during all activities, whether walking, standing, sitting, or lying down. Doing so will stop us from committing wrongful acts. *Eight Verses for Training the Mind* by Langri Thangpa is an ideal mind training text for this purpose, because it is both short and easy to memorize. By reciting such words of mind training, we remind ourselves that we want to avoid breaking our practice of training the mind.

AN ABSOLUTE ENLIGHTENED ATTITUDE

Having achieved stability, learn the secret.

First, train your mind well in the precious bodhicitta that constitutes the method. Then, when your familiarity with it is extremely stable, train in the precious absolute bodhicitta—wisdom inseparable from emptiness.

Having developed the relative enlightened attitude and made it stable, we should learn the secret, the meaning of emptiness, and then meditate on it until we realize it. Practicing in this way, we will eventually unify relative bodhicitta with absolute bodhicitta—the realization of emptiness.

Regard phenomena as dreamlike.

Reflect that things categorized as outer objects of perception are dreamlike because, aside from merely appearing to the mind as such, they do not have even an iota of true existence.

Reflect that all external phenomena—both the environment and living beings—are like dreams in that they appear to exist from their own side but do not have even the least bit of true existence. Although phenomena are merely labeled or imputed by the mind, they appear to us to be truly existent and on the basis of this appearance we then believe they actually do exist in this way.

Examine the nature of unborn awareness.

Reflect that things categorized as inner subjects that perceive are merely posited in dependence on the gathering or assemblage of their many respective causes and conditions. They do not independently apprehend, engage, or interact with objects. Therefore, they do not have even an iota of existence by way of their own entity.

Reflect, too, that all internal phenomena—subjects, i.e., the mind and mental states—are like dreams in that they are not born or produced from their own side but are merely imputed by thought.

In short, both objects (external phenomena) and subjects (internal phenomena) are like dreams.

The antidote itself is also free right where it is.

Then, ascertain that not only are those phenomena categorized as outer objects of perception and inner subjects that perceive not truly existent, but even suchness itself does not truly exist.

Outer objects, inner subjects, and even emptiness itself are not truly existent.

Focus on the nature of the basis of all, the entity of the path.

In purely etymological terms "the basis of all" refers to the basis on which uncontaminated imprints are deposited. But here it refers to emptiness, which is the basis of all of cyclic existence and nirvana. This is because when you realize emptiness you are able to attain the state of nirvana, but as long as you don't realize it you are not able to put an end to cyclic existence. Moreover, since any dependently-arisen thing appears out of emptiness, emptiness is like the basis for the arising of all of the dependently-related phenomena of cyclic existence and nirvana. Therefore cultivate the virtuous practice of meditative equipoise on the nature of emptiness.

The Cittamātra School[28] of Buddhist philosophy asserts an eighth type of consciousness, called "the basis of all."

It functions as the basis upon which all uncontaminated karmic imprints are deposited. However, the Prasaṅgika Madhyamaka School of Buddhist philosophy[29] does not accept the existence of such a consciousness. Instead, this school asserts that the basis of all is emptiness, the direct realization of which is essential for achieving nirvana. Because we are unable to achieve liberation from cyclic existence without the realization of emptiness, we should deepen our meditation on emptiness.

Between sessions be an illusionist.

Between meditation sessions maintain the illusory-like appearance that follows from meditation, in which all conventional phenomena appear even though they are empty. Reflect as follows:

> To an audience whose eyes have been affected by mantras or a magical salve, pebbles, sticks, and such can be made to appear as horses and oxen.[30] Nevertheless, pebbles, sticks, and such are not actually horses or oxen. Likewise, aside from merely appearing to be truly real under the polluting influence of imprints left by ignorance, all conventional phenomena do not truly exist.

During meditation sessions we focus our minds on emptiness. Then, in the interval between sessions we should maintain the understanding attained in meditation by considering all external phenomena to be like illusions conjured up by a magician. In other words, we should reflect that although the objects we perceive, such as trees and houses, appear to be truly real, they do not actually exist in this way. Illusions created by a magician with magical substances or mantras appear to be real horses, oxen, women, and so on, but the illusions are not in fact real horses and such. Similarly, we should reflect on the objects that appear to us following a session of meditation on emptiness as being illusion-like. In short, all our perceptions in the period between meditation sessions should be sustained by the understanding gained while absorbed in meditation on emptiness, the lack of true existence.

3: USING ADVERSITY ON THE PATH TO ENLIGHTENMENT

**When the container and its contents are filled with negativity,
transform adverse conditions into the path to enlightenment.**

Conditions in the world (the container) are such that the environmental consequences of the ten nonvirtues flourish: tree stumps, thorns, bits of brick, ravines, stones, and such abound. Similarly, conditions are such that the thoughts of sentient beings (the contents) are solely afflicted, their deeds are solely negative, and so on. The strength of gods and nāgas, who delight in goodness, is waning due to these conditions, while the strength of demons, malevolent forces, vengeful spirits, and elemental spirits who delight in evil is waxing. All religious people experience much harm as a result of this.

During this period in which we are entangled in unfavorable conditions, think of adverse conditions as favorable conditions, interference as assistance, and harmful beings, spirits, malevolent forces, and elemental spirits as virtuous friends. We transform adverse conditions into means for achieving enlightenment by doing so.

WE EXPERIENCE various unpleasant environmental conditions as a consequence of violating our ethical observance of the ten virtues[31] in the past. For example, the place where we are born may be filled with things like thorns, rough ground, rubbish, and deep ravines. Whatever faults we find in our environment are in fact the result of the wrongs we have committed in the past. Due to having acted nonvirtuously, we also personally experience unpleasant conditions, such as having to live with people whose thoughts are afflicted and whose deeds are nonvirtuous. In addition, when we allow our observance of ethical discipline to degenerate, gods and other beings on the side of virtue—who are themselves devoted to Dharma—grow unhappy and cease to help us. Instead, spirits and other beings on the side of nonvirtue grow more powerful and attempt to control and harm us. Human beings also harm us, and we experience illness and many other difficulties.

When such things happen, we as people who are training our minds must transform them into positive conditions, for this will allow us to gain spiritual realization. We can do so, for example, by choosing to see harmful beings as virtuous friends who are helping us to develop the enlightened attitude of bodhicitta. By practicing like this, we will be able to transform all adverse conditions into means for developing precious bodhicitta.

Immediately apply whatever you encounter to meditation.

In any circumstance whatsoever—whether in the monastery or in town, among humans or nonhumans; whether contented or suffering; whether things are good or bad, or you are facing sudden illness, spirits, enemies, and so on—no matter what terrible suffering befalls you, pray to your guru and the Three Jewels and do whatever training of your mind that you can.

Over the course of our lives we might live in a city, a small village, or even a monastery. We will meet all kinds of people, both good and bad, and may even come into contact with nonhuman spirits. At times we may experience the good life, while at others we may find ourselves in dire straits, like facing a serious illness or being harmed by spirits. We will also experience various feelings, sometimes being happy and at others unhappy. In all of these situations, we should remember and pray to our guru and the Three Jewels. Then we should immediately meditate on whatever problem we are experiencing so as to use it to develop bodhicitta.

The Four Practices

**To possess the four practices is the best
of methods.**

The first practice is to act virtuously. As soon as suffering comes and we wish to be free from it, we must put our effort into physical, verbal, and mental acts of virtue, such as offering things to the Three Jewels, serving the sangha, and giving ritual cakes to elemental spirits. After doing so we should pray to be blessed with sickness if it is better to be sick, to be blessed with a cure if it is better to be cured, and to be blessed with death if it is better to die. Be sure to make these requests with a mind in which hope and fear have been quieted.

The second practice is to confess our wrongs with the countermeasures of the four powers:

1. The power of total repudiation: to regret the wrongful deeds we have committed in the past;
2. The power of turning away from future wrongdoing: to resolve not to do wrong from now on, even at the cost of our lives;
3. The power of reliance: to seek refuge and develop the enlightened attitude of bodhicitta;
4. the power of administering antidotes: to meditate on emptiness, recite mantras, and so on.

The third practice is to make offerings to spirits. We must offer harmful beings, spirits, malevolent forces, and elemental spirits ritual cakes[32] while saying, "You are very kind because you help me train my mind. Once again give me the unwanted suffering of all mother sentient beings."

The fourth practice is to offer ritual cakes to Dharma protectors.[33] We must give them ritual cakes in accordance with the procedures followed by holy people of the past. Having performed such rituals as the ritual of one hundred offering cakes and the burnt flour ritual,[34] order the Dharma protectors to pacify conditions antagonistic to Dharma and to create favorable conditions. Also perform rites such as the rite of entrusting deeds, which enable us to make use of adverse conditions on the path to enlightenment.

ACTING VIRTUOUSLY

When we suffer we tend to wish to be free from it. This desire interferes with our practice of training the mind. We, as people who are training our minds, should not wish to be free even from situations of great suffering. Instead we should make all of our physical, verbal, and mental actions virtuous by praying that the Three Jewels bless us to be able to experience whatever will be of most benefit to our practice of Dharma: to be sick if it is better to be sick, to be cured if it is better to be cured, and to die if it is better to die.

We can also practice virtue by serving a spiritual community, such as a monastery or Dharma center, and by offering ritual cakes to the elemental spirits that belong to the realm of hungry ghosts. Whichever of these practices we choose to do, we should do it without any hope or fear. In other words, we shouldn't be too optimistic about completely recovering from serious illness, nor should we be too pessimistic about it definitely growing worse.

CONFESSING OUR WRONGS

The wrongs that we do vary in degree: some are heavier or more serious and others are lighter or less serious. Wrongful acts that are lighter include things like accidentally killing an insect, stealing a tiny worthless object, or telling a very small lie. The heaviest wrongs are those created by the mind—covetousness, malice, and wrong view. This is so because it is the mind that motivates us to act. Among these three types of mental wrongs, most of us probably do not have wrong views very often. Covetousness and malice, on the other hand, are more common and cause us to commit grave wrongdoing.

Malice—the wish to harm those whom we do not like—tends to come up more often than does covetousness. In some, malice is quite obvious, while in others it tends to be more concealed. Malice may vary even within a single person: it may sometimes be very weak, and at others very strong. Because we harm ourselves with malice much more than we do the people toward whom we develop it, it is wise to let go of malice rather than nourishing and mentally holding on to it. Another of the disadvantages of malice is that it even destroys virtue we amassed in our past lives, thereby making all of the time and energy that we put into acting virtuously a big waste. In fact, the reason that we should always dedicate our virtuous acts toward the attainment of enlightenment is to ensure that they will not be destroyed in the future by negative thoughts like malice.

In addition to confessing whatever wrongful acts we have committed in this immediate life, we must also purify the many wrongful acts—such as the five actions of immediate retribution[35]—that we've committed in previous lives.

The power of total repudiation

Knowing that if we do not confess our wrongful acts we will definitely be reborn into lower realms, we should develop a sense of regret for having committed such acts. This regret, here called "the power of total repudiation," should resemble the heartfelt regret that someone has when they realize that they have mistakenly ingested poisoned food.

We can liken the power of total repudiation to digging a trench around a tree and filling it with water in order to naturally weaken the roots of the tree so it will fall down. If we fervently regret having done wrong we will naturally wish to engage in the Dharma practices that remedy such acts, such as prostrating, offering, and praying. We become like someone who, having eaten poisoned food, is terrified of dying and urgently seeks a solution that will free them from that danger.

The power of turning away from future wrongdoing

In the past we didn't have the opportunity to meet a guru who could have taught us how to confess our wrongs. As a result we've done much wrong out of ignorance. Now that we know how to confess wrongdoings we should make a strong determination to not commit them ever again, even at the cost of our lives. This determination itself is the power of turning away from future wrongdoing. It may be the case, however, that we know that we cannot truthfully swear that we will never repeat a specific wrongful act again. We may even know that there is a good likelihood that we will do it again as soon as tomorrow. In such cases Kyabje Trijang Rinpoche, junior tutor to His Holiness the Fourteenth Dalai Lama, advised us to, at the very least, resolve not to do it again today.

The power of reliance

The power of reliance is comprised of taking refuge in the Three Jewels and developing an enlightened attitude toward all sentient beings. It is called "reliance" because taking refuge and developing bodhicitta purify wrongs done in reliance on the Three Jewels and other sentient beings, respectively.

When we take refuge and develop the enlightened attitude of bodhicitta, it isn't enough to merely repeat the words of a particular prayer; rather, we should do so from the depths of our hearts. This way these practices will be much more meaningful.

The power of administering antidotes

The power of administering antidotes consists of things like doing prostrations, presenting offerings, reciting mantras and prayers, and meditating on emptiness. Doing these things is "to administer antidotes" because these are the actual antidotes that we administer to purify our wrongful acts.

We compared the power of total repudiation to filling a ditch around the base of a tree with water in order to make the tree fall down. But that action doesn't have much power in itself. The power of administering antidotes, however, can be compared to using an ax to actually cut the tree down. In other words, when we use this power we engage in a practice that directly purifies our wrongful acts.

Although it is essential that all four powers are present when confessing wrongs, the two most important ones are the power of total repudiation and the power of turning way from future wrongdoing. When we have regret and determination like that we will automatically confess our negative actions. In short, by appreciating the benefits of these four powers we will naturally find the energy to use them. In the end, the efficacy of our practice of purification depends very much on our minds, for not only does the mind motivate us to act wrongly, it is the mind that confesses and purifies those acts.

I place a lot of emphasis on the practice of confession here because we can sometimes be a bit careless about this practice, and such carelessness is a big mistake. It is extremely important to confess our wrongs because higher states of realization can only be achieved after having confessed and purified our wrongful acts.

GIVING OFFERINGS TO SPIRITS

Instead of seeking revenge when evil spirits harm us, we should offer them things such as ritual cakes as a sign of our gratitude. When we do such practices we should think, "Thank you for the harm you have given me, because thereby you have helped me to develop the enlightened attitude of bodhicitta. Please continue to cause me even more problems and suffering in the future so that I will have many more occasions to train my mind."

OFFERING RITUAL CAKES TO DHARMA PROTECTORS

The holy people of the past made offerings to their own specific Dharma protectors so as to receive help from them in their spiritual practice. We, too, must entrust the protectors of Dharma with helping us to train our minds in the enlightened attitude by offering ritual cakes and other types of offering to them. We should ask for their help as we offer such things, saying, "O protectors of the Dharma! Enable me to bring all of the difficult conditions in my life onto the path to enlightenment, and grant me the perfect conditions to practice Dharma."

Aside from practicing training the mind, some people also do rituals and recite prayers to avoid experiencing problems, such as illness. But to authentically practice training the mind, we should willingly take any suffering that occurs upon ourselves. We should think, "Earlier when practicing 'taking and giving' I prayed that I would be able to take the suffering of other beings upon myself and that I would be able to give my happiness away to them. The suffering I experience now is their suffering that I prayed to take on." Thinking along these lines, we should be glad that our prayers have been answered. We can also joyfully make use of this opportunity by thinking, "May all other living beings be freed from illness by my experiencing this illness now."

To train the mind it is not enough to just know the words of a particular text. Rather, it is essential that we develop a deep understanding of its meaning and ponder it again and again. If we do this, our practice of training the mind will develop into a strong and stable foundation on which to gain higher spiritual realization. In fact, training the mind is like the first step in our Dharma practice: having developed facility in it, we can then progress to higher practices. To reach the top rung of a ladder we begin by climbing up the first rung and then continue on until we safely reach the top. Similarly, we will only reach the consummation of our practice of the Dharma by successfully accomplishing each step, one at a time.

4: A LIFETIME'S PRACTICE SUMMARIZED

THE FIVE POWERS: THE HEART OF TRAINING THE MIND

The summarized essence of the instructions is: apply yourself to the five powers.

The essence of the instructions is, in sum, to practice the five powers:

The Power of Resolve
Make a strong determination, thinking, "From this very day until I attain buddhahood or until I die, destroying the burgeoning afflictions of this month and this year, I will never allow my body, speech, or mind to stray from the instructions for training the mind in bodhicitta."

The Power of Familiarity
Make an effort to repeatedly and continuously familiarize and acquaint yourself with the attitude that you will quickly develop precious bodhicitta.

The Power of the Positive Seed
Strive to complete the two accumulations.[36] We accumulate merit by cultivating generosity, ethical discipline, and so on, which are the causes for the precious enlightened attitude that has yet to develop, for an enlightened attitude that has already been developed to remain, and for a lasting enlightened attitude to grow. We accumulate wisdom by cultivating meditative concentration and the understanding of emptiness.

The Power of Eradication
Continuously strive to administer the antidote to eradicate and do away with selfishness by seeing the disadvantages of cherishing yourself while neglecting others.

The Power of Prayer
Make fervent prayers dedicating your virtue, thinking, "By the strength of the roots of virtue I amass with body, speech, and mind in the past, present, and future may the precious enlightened attitude grow and grow."

It is said that these five powers, which summarize the entirety of Mahāyāna Dharma, can be encapsulated in a single syllable *hum*.

The power of resolve
The power of resolve is to strongly determine never to allow ourselves to stray from the instructions on training

the mind. In other words, we must never allow ourselves to stray from bodhicitta. To this end we must firmly decide, "From this moment until I attain enlightenment, or at least until I die, I will destroy all of the various kinds of afflictions, this very year, this very month." Although the term "affliction" generally refers to mental obscurations that obstruct our attainment of liberation, in this context it refers specifically to an attitude of cherishing oneself and neglecting others. So in this case "destroying afflictions" means to gain some control or power over our self-centeredness. Just as we successfully extinguish a fire if we forcefully overwhelm it, we should immediately attempt to forcefully overwhelm and put a stop to our sense of self-importance as soon as we notice it.

To train ourselves to cherish others, we should mentally take upon ourselves all the suffering that has yet to come to fruition for other sentient beings. When doing physical activities like prostrations, presenting offerings, or working for some Dharma purpose, for example, we should think that by doing so we are creating the causes for the suffering of other living beings to come to fruition on ourselves. We can also think this way as we do verbal activities like saying prayers or reciting mantras, and when we do mental activities like meditating on bodhicitta and emptiness. We should imagine that other sentient beings are freed from all their problems as a result of our practicing in this way.

By constantly keeping in mind an attitude that cherishes others, our development of bodhicitta will be continuous. Developing such positive thoughts is the actual practice of training the mind.

The power of familiarity

The power of familiarity is to repeatedly familiarize and acquaint ourselves with the enlightened attitude until it continuously and spontaneously occurs. To do this, we must concentrate initially on becoming very familiar with the practices for training the mind. In this way the practices will gradually become easier and easier until one day we will actually generate an enlightened attitude of bodhicitta.

The power of the positive seed

The power of the positive seed is to develop an enlightened attitude when one has yet to develop it, to make it firm once it has been developed, and to strengthen it once it has been made firm. To this end, we must take up practicing the six perfections—generosity, ethical discipline, patience, joyous effort, meditative concentration, and wisdom. The first five perfections belong to the practice of accumulating merit, while the last, the perfection of wisdom, belongs to the practice of accumulating wisdom. Supported by the strength of these two accumulations, we will be able to increase the strength of our bodhicitta.

If we want to take up the practice of generosity, we must first develop an attitude that wishes to give. On the basis of that attitude, we should begin to give what we have to others. Since it is not always easy to give away our belongings at first, we can begin in a gradual way. Someone who is extremely tightfisted, for example, can begin with something as simple as holding a small object in the right hand, passing it to the left hand, and then passing it back again while thinking, "I now give this object to my left hand. I now give it to my right."

There is a story in a sutra that illustrates just how miserly people can be.

There was once an arhat whose mother was quite rich but very stingy. Even though she was wealthy, she did not eat properly nor did she enjoy her many possessions. Furthermore, she was unable to give away even the tiniest thing. The arhat, knowing that if his mother did not change her behavior she would be reborn as a hungry ghost, advised her to offer something to the Three Jewels. In spite of her son's wise advice, the miserly woman was still reluctant to give away anything at all. After unsuccessfully admonishing her many times, the arhat finally gave her one of the scraps of yellow cloth used to make the robes worn by fully ordained monks. He then accompanied her to offer it to Śākyamuni Buddha. Although she did manage to offer the cloth to the Buddha, she stole it back the very same evening! The next day her son once again made her offer the scrap to the Buddha, but she again stole it back that evening! In desperation, after convincing his mother to offer the cloth once more, the arhat cut up the piece of cloth and sewed its bits and pieces onto the cushions that belonged to the monastic community. This time his mother did not take the cloth back—it was no longer of any use to her!

Reflecting on this and other examples of miserliness, we should try to be more generous and less tightfisted. People who possess plenty of material things can use whatever they need for themselves, but they should, at the very least, offer whatever they do not use to the Three Jewels or give it to the poor. If they do not do this they will create the causes to be born as hungry ghosts.

When practicing generosity and the other perfections, we should always remember how very fortunate we are to have this opportunity. In fact, we have all the tools—the methods, knowledge, material objects, and so forth—needed to accumulate merit and wisdom.

The power of eradication
The power of eradication is to eradicate selfish thoughts—those that make us look down on and neglect others while cherishing ourselves. We should apply antidotes to our self-centeredness by contemplating the disadvantages of cherishing ourselves and the advantages of cherishing others. Recall that a self-important attitude causes us much suffering and many problems, while an attitude that cherishes others brings us great benefit and happiness. Having understood this, we should work to gradually do away with selfishness.

The power of prayer
The power of prayer is to dedicate all the physical, verbal, and mental virtues that we have created in the past, that we are creating in the present, and that we will create in the future to the development of an enlightened attitude for

the sake of all sentient beings. We physically create virtue by doing prostrations, circumambulating monasteries and stupas, and other such activities. We verbally accumulate virtue by reciting mantras, prayers, and so forth. And we mentally create virtue by doing practices like meditating on emptiness.

The five powers summarize all the Mahāyāna instructions and a lifetime's practice of Dharma is summarized by the practice of the five powers. It is said that the practice of the five powers can be encapsulated in a single syllable *hum*.

The Mahāyāna Instructions for Transferring Consciousness

The Mahāyāna instructions for transferring consciousness are precisely these five powers; ...

The Instruction of the Positive Seed
Sell without clinging whatever belongings you have and then liberally offer things to the sources of greatest merit, such as the Three Jewels.

The Instruction of Prayer
Offer the seven-part prayer[37] to your guru and the Three Jewels and then fervently pray, "May I, in the intermediate state[38] and in all my lives, never be parted from the two types of precious bodhicitta. Bless me especially to meet a guru who will reveal this Dharma to me."

The Instruction of Eradication
Since you have been caused to suffer in the past and are still being made to suffer now as a result of not having done away with clinging to your body, possessions, friends, relatives, and so on, and holding tightly to them instead, do away with and eradicate clinging even to your body and life.

The Instruction of Resolve
Develop a strong aspiration, thinking, "I will train in precious bodhicitta even in the intermediate state."

The Instruction of Familiarity
When it is time to die, lie on your right side in the leonine posture. Block your right nostril with the ring finger of your right hand and fervently practice taking and giving as you breathe in and out. In addition, stop grasping at true existence by reflecting that cyclic existence and nirvana, birth and death, and such are nothing other than just appearances to a mistaken mind and do not exist by their own nature. You should be able to die while alternately meditating on the two kinds of precious bodhicitta in this way.

The five Mahāyāna instructions on transferring consciousness[39] should be practiced only when we are certain that death is imminent.

The instruction of the positive seed

As we near death it is important to diminish our tendency to cling to our belongings by giving them away. We can give them to superior recipients, such as the Three Jewels, or to inferior ones, such as the poor and the needy. If we don't do this, attachment to our possessions will prevent us from making progress on the spiritual path, like a chain bound around our ankles prevents us from walking.

Furthermore, when actually dying it is best not to worry at that point about making a will, as this could aggravate attachment and clinging to our possessions. It is best to make a will while still healthy and free of mental and physical problems, because it is best to die calmly, with as little talk as possible. In addition, we should not be preoccupied with eating when dying, nor should our friends and relatives encourage us to eat. Most importantly, we should be free from sadness, regret, and discouraging thoughts, such as thinking that we did not accomplish anything worthwhile during our lives. If we approach death in the right way, we will be able to die peacefully and without excessive worry about where we will be reborn.

It is said that we receive our Dharma practice "grades" when we are dying. Only when the subtle mind is about to leave the physical body do we find out how well we have actually practiced. Excellent practitioners joyfully experience death, as though returning home with a happy mind, average practitioners experience death free of regret and worry, and those who have practiced very little experience a great reluctance to die, as well as fear and anxiety.

The instruction of prayer

When we are very close to death, weak and no longer able to move, it is very important to offer up prayers, like the seven-part prayer, to the Three Jewels. We should also specifically pray that, as we pass between lives and in all our future lives, we may never be parted from the two types of precious bodhicitta and that we may always have the good fortune to meet gurus who teach the holy Dharma.

The instruction of eradication

Dying people generally find themselves surrounded by sad and weeping relatives and friends, which causes attachment to arise in their hearts. However, it is very important when we are close to death to not be attached to our parents, relatives, and friends, or even to our own bodies. To diminish this attachment we should think, "As a result of attachment to relatives, friends, and others in past lives, I have been reborn again and again in the cycle of existence and in all my lives I have continually had to experience various kinds of suffering. If I am once again unable to give up such attachment, it will only bring me further rebirths and more suffering in cyclic existence." Thinking in this way we will be able to completely cut off attachment when we are dying.

It is also advisable that the person dying not look around too much at the people around them so as to diminish their attachment. Instead, it is best if we keep our eyes closed and maintain a peaceful mental state by meditating on bodhicitta and praying to the Three Jewels.

The instruction of resolve

At the time of death, when the mind is about to depart from the body, we should strongly resolve never to give up the practices of training the mind and to continue to train our minds in bodhicitta even in the intermediate state.

The instruction of familiarity

When dying, we should lie in the leonine posture, as did Śākyamuni Buddha: lay on the right side, with the palm of the right hand under the right cheek, both legs almost fully extended, and the left arm resting atop the left side of the body. Lying in that posture we should then alternately meditate on the two kinds of bodhicitta. We can do so by practicing taking and giving at times, and by eliminating grasping at true existence at others by contemplating the fact that death and rebirth are like illusions.

At the time of death it is generally taught that we should block our right nostril with our right ring finger to stop the flow of nonvirtuous winds, or energies.[40] However, those who are training their minds by combining the practice of taking and giving with the inhalation and exhalation of the breath can omit blocking the right nostril.

... cherish this conduct.

With respect to how to conduct oneself at the point of death, it is extremely important not to stray from the five powers, the Mahāyāna instructions for transferring consciousness. Thus, be certain to carefully exert yourself in practicing them. Since the signs of continuous and successful Dharma practice will become evident at that time, develop the ability to die in a state of contentment thinking, "Even if I have to remain in the dark hole of the Hell of Unrelenting Torment in order to secure the welfare of all my mother sentient beings of old, I will gladly do so."

Here "conduct" refers to the practices for training the mind that we must cherish particularly at the time of death. When dying we learn how skilled we have become at bodhicitta by practicing the five powers during our life. If we have trained the mind, then when we are about to die we will be neither worried nor pray, "May I never be reborn in hell and may I always experience happiness." Instead, we will be able to pray, "May I be reborn in hell for the sake of all my mother sentient beings who are tormented there."

The five powers, the Mahāyāna instructions for transferring consciousness, should not be taken lightly. Instead, we should take these instructions to heart and strive to put the five powers into practice in our daily life as much as possible.

5: THE MEASURE OF A TRAINED MIND

Gather all Dharmas into one intent.

Since all Mahāyāna and Hinayāna Dharmas were taught solely as antidotes to selfishness, the measure of our practice of Dharma is the extent to which our practice has acted as an antidote to our own selfishness. This is also the scale upon which people who practice Dharma are weighed.

ANYTHING THAT ACTS as an antidote to selfishness is a Dharma practice. So even though we may engage in a great variety of practices that appear to be spiritual in nature, if they fail to do away with our selfishness, they are not Dharma practices. This measure of our success in having trained the mind is also said to be the scale that weighs whether we truly practice Dharma or not.

Of the two witnesses uphold the main one.

Although the untroubled minds of others might be suitable witnesses for our practice, because it is possible that a mere show of good behavior can please ordinary worldly people, don't rely on them as your primary witness. The Three Jewels see you clearly and without impediment at all times, day and night. As there is nothing whatsoever that they and your guru do not know about, always avoid hypocrisy.

You are your main witness because you cannot conceal your own heart from yourself. Given that you cannot lie to yourself, fool yourself, or make a mockery of yourself, you are your own main witness. This too is a measure of having trained your mind.

Other people are one type of witness to our practice of training the mind, but our own hearts are another. Other people witness how we behave: when we do wrong they criticize us, and when we do right they praise and respect us. But it is possible that although our physical and verbal behavior appears to be quite good, our hearts—the main witness of our practice—may actually be overwhelmed by one of the three poisons of attachment, hatred, or ignorance. If our hearts are filled with any of these poisons and we do not acknowledge it, regardless of how good we may appear to others, we will just be lying to ourselves. We deceive ourselves with this behavior because although we may succeed in getting what we want in this life, we utterly destroy our own happiness in future lives by acting contrary to Dharma.

On the other hand, if we knowingly act nonvirtuously without trying to get our minds under control, we deceive and displease the Three Jewels, who see our minds and our every action. For this reason, the Three Jewels and our gurus, who embody the Three Jewels, can also be considered main witnesses.

We should take care not to deceive other people, our outer witnesses, by pretending to practice Dharma, and we should be equally concerned not to deceive ourselves or our gurus, our inner witnesses. In sum, when training in the enlightened attitude of bodhicitta it is essential that we avoid hypocrisy. Rather than acting one way while thinking differently in our hearts, we should always act sincerely. This too is a measure that accurately indicates how much progress we have made in training the mind.

Always rely on a happy mind alone.

Whenever others falsely criticize you even though you haven't done anything wrong, whenever you experience physical or mental illnesses and pain—in short, whenever any undesired suffering occurs—delight in it, thinking, "I can bring this experience onto my path of training the mind without allowing my training of the mind to deteriorate." Strengthen your resolve in this way. When you have this attitude, your mind is trained.

At times others may scold, curse, blame, belittle, or accuse us even though we haven't done anything wrong. Or at times we may become temporarily sick or even contract a serious life-threatening illness. But if we are sincerely training our minds, we should not let these experiences make us unhappy. Instead, we should remain happy by accepting suffering and looking at it as an excellent opportunity to further train our minds. The ability to willingly accept and endure suffering is another measure that indicates how much we have trained our minds.

The measure of being trained is to no longer regress.

Proceed from the preliminary Dharma practices in the beginning—the contemplations of the meaningfulness of the freedom and opportunity that this precious human life affords, the difficulty of obtaining it, and so on—up to training in the absolute enlightened attitude of bodhicitta. The measure of being trained in each of these preliminary practices is to no longer regress. When, for example, you no longer squander the freedom and opportunity that you have, regardless of circumstances, and have developed in your heart a genuine attitude capable of extracting the essence of this precious human life, then your mind is trained in that practice.

Initially we should train our minds by contemplating things like the meaningfulness of this precious human life, death and impermanence, and so on. In other words, we must first train in the stages of the path for people of lesser capability and then in those for people of middling capability. Only after we have trained ourselves in these two paths should we begin to train in the enlightened attitude of bodhicitta. Developing our practice gradually in this way, we will steadily progress at training the mind without any regression.

THE FIVE GREATNESSES

The sign of being trained is to be great in five ways.

Do not be without the five greatnesses. Be a great bodhisattva: seeing that the precious Mahāyāna enlightened attitude of bodhicitta is the essence of all the scriptures, train in it at all times. Be a great observer of ethical discipline: having gained conviction in the law of actions and their consequences, shun even the slightest faulty act. Be a great ascetic: endure hardships in order to destroy the afflictions in your heart. Be a great student of virtue: never let your physical or verbal actions stray from the ten acts of Mahāyāna Dharma.[41] And be a great yogi: continuously cultivate the yogas that prevent precious bodhicitta and its contributing factors from degenerating.[42]

A great bodhisattva
The first sign of having successfully trained the mind is to become a great bodhisattva who, having come to understand that the enlightened attitude of bodhicitta is the

essence of all the Mahāyāna teachings, constantly trains in and develops it.

A great observer of ethical discipline

The second sign of having trained the mind is to become a great observer of ethical discipline who, having belief in and respect for the law of actions and their consequences, avoids doing even the slightest wrong, such as killing an ant or making a rude gesture, due to knowing that such acts will bring suffering as their future consequence.

A great ascetic

The third sign of having trained the mind is to become a great ascetic who is able to bear any hardship for the purpose of destroying afflictions.

A great student of virtue

The fourth sign of having trained the mind is to become a great student of virtue who, in all their physical and verbal actions, never strays from the ten Dharma acts that are the Mahāyāna practice.

A great yogi

The fifth sign of having trained the mind is to become a great yogi who constantly cultivates precious bodhicitta by undertaking the trainings that are the causes that produce it, such as contemplating the sevenfold cause and effect technique.[43]

**If this can be done even when distracted,
you are trained.**

An expert horseman never falls from their horse even when distracted. Similarly, being able to transform unpleasant experiences into aids for training the mind without becoming angry is a measure of having successfully trained your mind. For example, when someone speaks to you in an undesirable fashion—addressing you contemptuously, verbally abusing you, swearing at you, deriding you, or falsely accusing you—you think in response, "Even the Buddha himself had many such experiences; this is a result of my own wrongful deeds due to not having done away with malice."

A person who has genuinely trained their mind is comparable to an experienced horseman who, even though distracted, does not fall from a galloping wild horse. Similarly, a person who is well trained in the enlightened attitude of bodhicitta is able to tolerate problems caused by other people and to transform such seemingly difficult conditions into means for developing their bodhicitta.

For example, when criticized or wrongly blamed a practitioner of mind training doesn't get angry. Instead they reflect, "Even the Buddha, who was omniscient, was criticized and disparaged by other people, including his cousin Devadatta. But I am a very ordinary and insignificant person compared to someone like the Buddha. The only reason that people harm, criticize, and accuse me in this life is that I didn't do away with malice in the past."

In short, our ability to bear difficulties and transform them into means for strengthening our enlightened attitude is a measure of how well we have trained our minds.

6: THE COMMITMENTS OF MIND TRAINING

Constantly train in three general points.

Do not contradict the commitments of mind training. In other words, don't overlook even the most minor training.

Do not be reckless. Don't behave recklessly by digging up the ground, cutting down trees, or disturbing water where spirits live,[44] or by going to disease-ridden areas rather than avoiding them, and so on.

Do not be biased. Avoid the three types of bias: tolerating harm from humans while not tolerating harm from gods or spirits, being patient with superiors but disparaging inferiors, and being affectionate toward friends but hating enemies.

THE FIRST COMMITMENT of mind training is to very carefully observe all eighteen of the mind training commitments without contradicting even the most minor one. Since those who train in bodhicitta will, in general, have taken bodhisattva vows, this first commitment also includes not violating the eighteen root and forty-six secondary bodhisattva vows.[45]

The second commitment of mind training is a commitment not to be reckless or arrogant by thinking, for example, that due to our level of spiritual realization we can do whatever we like, such as digging up the earth where nāgas live, cutting down trees inhabited by spirits, or being careless when visiting people with contagious diseases. When training the mind we should never arrogantly show other people that we have attained realization or tell them that we have developed bodhicitta.

The third commitment of mind training is a commitment to avoid being biased toward others. We might be able to endure harm from human beings but find it difficult to tolerate harm from evil spirits, against whom we might perform various destructive rituals; or we might be able to bear being humiliated by a wealthy or powerful person but not be able to bear being despised or belittled by a person whom we consider to be inferior to us in some way; or we may be willing to help those who are our friends but not those whom we identify as enemies. However, since we are training our minds, we should act impartially toward everyone at all times.

Change your attitude while remaining as you are.

Having changed your attitude mentally, act in accordance with Mahāyāna mind training without any artifice. Inconspicuously and effectively mature your own mind, unperceived by others.

The fourth commitment of mind training is to change our attitudes without revealing our spiritual practice to others. While we may practice perfectly and achieve very good results, it is better to conceal our progress from others and to show only that we are practicing a little and have achieved minor results.

Don't speak of others' defects.

If others have defects, such as a handicap, blindness, deafness, dumbness, imperfect limbs, or even corrupted ethics, never mention them. Don't even criticize nonhuman beings by calling them names like "evil spirits." As *Rays of Sunlight Mind Training* says, "Give up wrathful rites of subjugation. Practice training your mind strongly."

Quell violent impulses toward nonhuman beings, for example, with love and compassion. Encouraging spirits intent on harm not to hurt others will plant in their minds the seed of liberation and become the cause of both your and their happiness. Otherwise you might use wrathful tantric practices to perform wrathful burnt offerings, wrathful offerings of ritual cakes, or wrathful rites for the suppression of spirits. But, in the short run, performing such rites causes many different illnesses to afflict both yourself and others and ensures that whatever you do will not become a spiritual path. In the long run, the spirits' resentment of you on account of your wrathful acts will hurt you in both this and future lives.

Similarly, when you speak gently to human beings, have good intentions toward them, and do what benefits them, whatever you do in this life will become a spiritual path and everyone will praise your behavior. Behaving thusly will become a cause of happiness in both this life and in future lives. Otherwise, you might harm others, directly or indirectly, with malicious speech, harsh words, evil intentions, deception, and so on. But if you do, in the short run, whatever you do will not become a spiritual path. And in both the short and long run, your behavior will only cause harm to yourself since everyone will think of you as their enemy.

So you should never wrathfully subjugate anyone in anger, human or otherwise. Instead, you must at all times and in every situation persist at wrathfully subjugating your own obstinate mind, without wavering.

The fifth commitment of mind training is to not speak of the defects of others, such as saying that they lack a particular quality or pointing out their impaired limbs. We should also not insult others by calling them disparaging names and such, as when we offend nonhuman spirits by calling them evil. If we do so, the insulting behavior, aside from interfering with our successfully training our minds, also runs the risk of leading the spirits to decide to wreak havoc by causing all kinds of problems for us. If this were to happen, we might in turn think to stop them with some type of wrathful practice, such as reciting mantras or offering ritual cakes. However, since such beings are clairvoyant they would know who is harming them, and would therefore come to hold a grudge and look for an opportunity to avenge themselves. So it would be much better if, right from the outset, we were to develop an attitude of loving kindness toward these spirits who, knowing our positive thoughts, would consequently help us.

We should also try to benefit human beings as much as possible because the outcome of such behavior is always positive in the long run. On the other hand, if we were to use our authority or harsh words to get what we want, while we might enjoy some success in the short run, in the future the people whom we've abused will likely harm us out of resentment.

In short, we should use aggressive means, not to destroy other sentient beings, but to destroy our own mental afflictions, particularly our self-centeredness. As Śāntideva clearly states in *Guide to the Bodhisattva's Way of Life*:

> When everyday enemies are banished from one
>   place,
> they retreat and settle in another.
> Then, having recouped their power, they come back.
> Afflictions, however, are not that kind of enemy.

Don't reflect on others' shortcomings.

Whenever we find fault in sentient beings in general, and in religious people in particular, we should do away with the attitude that conceives of such faults, thinking, "This is a result of things appearing impurely to me. How else could they have such faults?"

The sixth commitment of mind training is to give up seeking out and judging the faults in others, including those in religious people. Instead, we should train our minds to see others as pure by thinking that when we see a fault in someone, it's because we project imaginary faults onto others due to things appearing to be impure from our own side. Practicing in this way, we will be able to protect ourselves from the tendency to judge others.

First purify whatever affliction is strongest.

Examine which affliction in your mind is the strongest. Then, having amassed all the Dharma as its antidote, get rid of that one first. As *Rays of Sunlight Mind Training* says, "First purify whichever is coarsest."

The seventh commitment of mind training is to purify first whichever affliction is strongest in our mind. To do so, we must begin by examining the many kinds of affliction that come up in our mind. Once we have identified the predominant one, we should administer the antidote specific to it before going on to eliminate other less troubling afflictions.

Give up all hope of reward.

Don't think to attain liberation just to satisfy your own wish for happiness. Instead, strive to attain liberation for the welfare of all sentient beings, your former mothers.

The eighth commitment of mind training is to give up all hope and expectation of receiving some personal benefit from the practice of training the mind, like attaining liberation from cyclic existence just for ourselves. Instead, we should put all our effort into achieving the state of perfect complete enlightenment for the sake of other beings by constantly reminding ourselves that we are training our minds in order to help others find happiness.

Discard poisoned food.

Just as food will be fatal if mixed with poison, any virtue you do will actually be fatal to your liberation if it is mixed with grasping at true existence or an attitude of self-importance. Therefore, do not mix your roots of virtue with grasping at true existence or with self-centeredness.

The ninth commitment of mind training is to not mix virtue with a mistaken sense of self and an attitude of self-importance. When we act virtuously but with a mistaken sense of self or self-importance, those actions actually end up harming us by rending our virtues and preventing liberation, just as food endangers life when mixed with poison. So when we practice generosity toward the poor or toward the Three Jewels, for example, we should be extremely careful not to mix such positive acts with either the thought that things truly exist or the thought that we are more important than others. Instead, we should strive to completely rid ourselves of these two mental states.

Don't hold a grudge.

Give up forever clinging to vindictiveness once you've
developed enmity toward someone who has hurt you.

The tenth commitment of mind training is to give up holding grudges against those who have hurt us by physically
striking or verbally insulting us, for example. We should
always avoid cultivating vindictiveness and never make
plans for any future retaliation.

Don't mock with malicious sarcasm.

Even if others speak words that seem to nearly break
your heart, strive to say not a single harmful word in
response.

The eleventh commitment of mind training is to not use
harmful words in retaliation, even if others wound us
deeply by mocking, scolding, or speaking harshly to us.

Don't lie in ambush.

Don't behave in such a way that, because you deeply
resent the harm done to you by another, you retaliate
one day when the chance to avenge yourself finally
appears.

According to the twelfth commitment of mind training,
even if someone has hurt you and you did not immediately

retaliate, you should not wait, as though lying in ambush, for the chance to hurt them back.

Don't strike at the heart.

Don't spy out other people's faults, recite fatal mantras that would harm spirits, and so on.

The thirteenth commitment of mind training is to not reveal the faults and weaknesses of others, even if we know them, with the intent to cause them harm.

Don't put a horse's load on a pony.[46]

Do not divert onto others, by various devious means, the blame that should fall upon yourself.

The fourteenth commitment of mind training is to not point to others as the source of a mistake that we ourselves have made.

Don't sprint to win a race.

Don't say that you alone have benefited a person when you have done so with the help of others. And avoid using various means to get things for yourself alone when they are meant to be shared between yourself and others.

The fifteenth commitment of mind training is to not claim to have done a good thing alone when, in fact, others helped us to do it. In addition, we should not keep for ourselves valuable gifts given in common, deceitfully trying to avoid sharing them, when it was intended that they be shared between ourselves and others.

Don't misuse this practice as a rite.

Don't accept temporary defeat from others only out of a desire for your own eventual gain, and do not train your mind as a means of alleviating illness caused by spirits and such, because doing so would be practicing only to achieve trivial goals.

The sixteenth commitment of mind training is to not allow others to treat us badly now with the hope of receiving some kind of benefit later. We also should not train in the enlightened attitude of bodhicitta just to prevent spirits from harming us or to prevent the people we have harmed from retaliating. To behave in such a way would be to act like someone who misuses this profound practice as a rite for achieving trivial goals.

Don't turn a god into a demon.

"Turning a god into a demon" refers to making mistakes in the propitiation of a god to whom you have been devoted, thereby causing him to kill you. By way of analogy, if your pride, conceit, or hatred grow stron-

ger as a result of the cultivation of training the mind,
this would be like turning a god into a demon. Don't
allow this to happen.

The seventeenth commitment of mind training is to not
turn a god into a demon. This generally refers to a situation
in which, having previously propitiated some worldly god
or another to gain success, we make a mistake in our man-
ner of devotion, thereby causing that god to make problems and hurt us, like a demon. If, as a result of training in
the enlightened attitude of bodhicitta, we become more,
rather than less, afflicted by anger, pride, jealousy, and so
on, this is like turning a god into a demon.

Don't seek suffering as a means to happiness.

Give up wishing others suffer as a means to your own
happiness by thinking, for example, that the property
of your relatives, friends, companions in the Dharma,
or others, such as their food, wealth, and texts, will be
yours when they die; or that the fortune of a great
meditator will be yours alone when he dies since you
were associates; or that you will finally be free from
harm when your enemy dies.

The eighteenth commitment of mind training is to not
enjoy the happiness we gain at the expense of the suffering of others. We should not, for example, rejoice when
relatives or friends die, thinking that we will now receive
their property. Nor should we rejoice when someone more

famous than ourselves dies, thinking that we will now get their position or title. Likewise, we should not rejoice when our enemies die, thinking how great it is that no one is left to harm us now.

7: THE PRECEPTS OF MIND TRAINING

Do all yogas single-mindedly.

Everything you do—eating, dressing, walking, standing, lying, and sitting—should be sustained by the sole intention to benefit others.

WE OUGHT TO DO all yogas, or activities, single-mindedly with the enlightened attitude. In other words, we must never stray from bodhicitta no matter what we are doing.

Overcome all misguiding influences with one.

Whenever you do not feel a heartfelt desire to train your mind, if, for example, you have been harmed by spirits or your mind is strongly afflicted, turn away from the influence of such misguided thoughts and redouble your enthusiasm for training the mind.

Instead of being discouraged whenever we encounter problems like sickness, spirit harm, or strong afflictions, we should inspire ourselves and build our courage by remembering that such situations are quite useful for developing an enlightened attitude. Thinking in this way, we make all of our difficulties into conditions that will help us to have the energy and enthusiasm needed to bring our practice of training the mind to completion.

There are two acts: one at the beginning and one at the end.

The two acts of developing a noble motivation at the beginning of the day and making dedicatory prayers at the end are equally important. As soon as you wake up in the morning make a resolution, thinking, "Today, without straying from the two precious enlightened attitudes, I will make meaningful the freedom and opportunity that I have." Use mindfulness and vigilance to keep this motivation throughout the day. At night examine your heart as you go to sleep. If you find that you did not contradict the practice of training your mind during the day, feel glad about it. Also think, "Tomorrow, without straying from the practice of training my mind, I will make meaningful the freedom and opportunity that I have."

Those who are training their minds should always remember to begin each day by bringing up a positive motivation and to end each day by dedicating whatever merit they have created. So when we wake up in the morning, we should give rise to the enlightened attitude of bodhicitta, thinking, "Today I will take full advantage of this precious human life, as much as I can, without straying from the enlightened attitude." Then throughout the day we should continuously rely on mindfulness and vigilance to examine whether or not we are really keeping an enlightened attitude of bodhicitta as our motivation. At night, before going to sleep, we should examine the various things that we have done throughout the day to determine whether or not we really trained ourselves in the enlightened attitude. If we find that we did something that was not in keeping with the practice of training our minds, we should confess it right away and purify it with the four opponent powers. On the other hand, if we find that we did not contradict our practice of training the mind, but acted virtuously, we should congratulate ourselves. Finally, just before going to sleep, we should strongly determine to continue the practice of training the mind the following day.

Bear whichever of the two arises.

If you are particularly well-off or have a lot of property, think of wealth as being illusion-like and use it, without arrogance, to benefit others as much as you can. On the other hand, if you are depressed and think, "I am the lowest of the low," train your mind in the precious enlightened attitude by taking the depression of other living beings onto yourself, without discouragement.

We may experience very different situations over the course of our lives. We might be rich and famous at one point and find ourselves poor and lonely at another. When things are going well, rather than being arrogant or conceited about it, we should reflect that wealth, property, fame, and such are like illusions and use them to benefit others. On the other hand, when things are going badly, we should patiently endure the situation without becoming depressed and cheer ourselves up by thinking how fortunate we are to have this precious human life.

Guard two at the cost of your life.

Since the commitments of Dharma, in general, and the commitments of mind training, in particular, are fundamental, guard them even more dearly than you do your life.

The commitments of Dharma include the vows of personal liberation, the bodhisattva vows, and the tantric vows.[47] The commitments of mind training are the eighteen commitments of mind training that support our practice of cherishing others more than ourselves. We should keep these two types of commitments even at the cost of our lives.

Train in three difficulties.

As it is difficult to be mindful of afflictions at the beginning, identify them. As it is difficult to counteract afflictions in the middle, develop the strength of effective mental antidotes and strive to counteract them. As it is difficult to sever the flow of afflictions at the end, contemplate their disadvantages from many angles and thereby sever their continuity.

In the beginning it is difficult to identify or recognize the afflictions. Later it is difficult to avert them. And in the end it is very difficult to sever their flow—or in other words, to eliminate them completely.

When things went wrong before we began to train our minds our tendency was to point to factors outside of ourselves as the source of our problems. This is why it is difficult in the beginning to recognize that our own sense of self-importance and our afflictions are responsible for our problems and flaws. But even after we learn to recognize our afflictions, it is still very difficult to avert them because we are unable to administer strong and effective antidotes to counteract them when they arise. And later, even though we may gain the ability to avert afflictions, it is still difficult to totally eradicate them from our minds.

Therefore, it is important at this point to refer to relevant scriptures and to use reason to examine the disadvantages of the afflictions in many ways. We may reflect, for example, that mental affliction has caused us to be repeatedly reborn into the cycle of existence, and that if we do not eliminate it now, we will also be caused to be endlessly reborn here in the future. With thoughts like these we should strongly determine to eliminate the afflictions once and for all.

Adopt three principal causes.

The three principal causes or conditions are: the external condition—meeting an excellent guru who teaches the Mahāyāna path without error; the internal condition—a qualified mind that, having acquired a body possessed of freedom and opportunity, has faith and is replete with wisdom, joyous effort, and so on; and the assemblage of conditions amenable to the accomplishment of Dharma without falling to extremes with respect to resources.

If these three principal causes are complete, be happy. If they are incomplete, put effort into creating the causes for completing them and pray from the depths of your heart that they might be quickly completed.

There are three principal causes, or conditions, that allow us to train the mind. The first is to have met a qualified guru capable of correctly teaching us the path to enlightenment without error. The second is to have the right internal conditions: the freedom and opportunity of a precious human life and its attendant intelligence and wisdom. The third is to live moderately without falling to the extremes of either leading an excessively hedonistic life distracted by having too much of everything or of leading an excessively ascetic life plagued by the difficulties associated with lack of basic necessities.

We should check to see if we presently possess these three causes of successful spiritual practice. If we find that we have them, we should be happy and take advantage of our fortunate situation. If we find that we do not have them, we should work at creating the causes to acquire them.

Cultivate three without allowing them to deteriorate.

Do all three of the following: don't allow your appreciation of and respect for your guru to deteriorate, since he is the principal cause of developing qualities; don't allow your enthusiasm for training the mind to deteriorate; and don't allow your mind to stray from the two types of precious bodhicitta.

We should never allow our faith and respect for the guru to deteriorate, because the guru is the source of our every good quality. Second, we should never allow our enthusiasm, joy, and courage for training the mind to deteriorate. And third, we should never allow ourselves to stray from the two kinds of enlightened attitude, the relative and the absolute.

Possess three inseparably.

Never physically, verbally, or mentally stray from acting virtuously.

Do not physically stray from doing acts like prostrating, presenting offerings, offering mandalas, or circumambulating. Do not verbally stray from reciting prayers, mantras, or verses for training the mind. And do not mentally stray from cultivating the two enlightened attitudes, the cause for accumulating the merit and wisdom needed to attain the mind and body of a buddha.[48]

Train in purity and impartiality with respect to objects.

Train your mind to see purity with respect to both living beings and inanimate objects. Train your mind to be impartial.

We should train ourselves to be impartial with respect to objects, whether animate or inanimate, by training ourselves to see things as pure. To do this we must stop identifying some things as attractive and others as repulsive, which we can do by seeing our environment as a pure land and all living beings as its resident gods and goddesses.

Train inclusively and profoundly: cherish all.

Impartially train your mind with regard to sentient beings born in four ways. Include everyone you see in your training of the mind so that your mind training becomes more than just words.

The four ways in which sentient beings are born cover the varieties of birth: from a womb, from an egg, from heat and moisture, and by way of miracle. We should impartially train ourselves to cherish every sentient being born in these various ways.

Ever acquaint yourself with special cases.

There are five special cases you must acquaint yourself with: since the Three Jewels, your gurus, and your parents are very kind to you and are particularly sensitive referents of your actions, do not get angry with them; although the members of your family with whom you constantly associate may give you many reasons to get angry with them, do not react with anger to them; avoid getting angry with those who compete with you, whether they are lay men or women, monks or nuns; if harmful beings turn against you even though you have done nothing to them, do not get angry with them; and if you find yourself becoming repulsed or angry just by hearing the name or seeing the face of a person in spite of never before having been acquainted or intimate with them, cultivate an especially affectionate love for them.

In terms of special cases, the first is to not get angry with those who are our superiors—the Three Jewels, our gurus, and our parents. The second is to not get angry with the people we live with—our partners, parents, and friends. The third is to not get angry with anyone who competes with us, whether lay or ordained. The fourth is to not get angry with those who harm us even though we have done no harm to them. And the fifth is to cultivate love for those who we feel unhappy or uncomfortable with by just hearing their names or seeing them from a distance.

Don't depend on other conditions.

Train your mind when enjoying favorable conditions, such as having sufficient food and clothing, being free from harm by humans and nonhumans, and being in good health. But even when not enjoying favorable conditions, do not stop training your mind. You must continue to train your mind.

Our practice of mind training should not depend on external conditions such that when we have plenty of food, clothing, and so on we practice training the mind, but when we lack them we do not. In short, we should always practice mind training, whether we are experiencing favorable conditions or not.

Take up what is most important right now.

Until today, there has been no meaning to our taking up body after body throughout lifetimes without beginning. Now, having understood that between talking about training the mind and doing it, doing it is most important, you should do nothing but train the mind.

We have had many different kinds of lives in the past, but those lives were meaningless because we wasted them. Now that we have gained a precious human life brimming with valuable potential, we should immediately use it to put the mind training that we have studied into practice so as to actually accomplish the transformation of our mind.

Avoid understanding wrongly.

Avoid six types of wrong understanding: to lack the patience to bear hardships for the sake of Dharma, while patiently bearing hardships in order to overcome your enemies and protect your friends, is to wrongly understand patience; to not aspire to accomplish Dharma, while aspiring to happiness and comfort in this life, is to wrongly understand aspiration; to not savor listening to the Dharma, thinking about it, and meditating on it, while savoring the worldly happiness produced by attachment, hatred, and ignorance, is to wrongly understand savoring; to not cultivate compassion for sentient beings tormented by suffering, while cultivating compassion for religious people when you see they lack a trifling bit of food or clothing, is to wrongly understand compassion; to not lead your friends and relatives to Dharma, while leading them to manage donations made to the Three Jewels and the Sangha, which can be misused, and teaching them methods for getting rich in this life, is to wrongly understand a caring attitude; and to not rejoice for the roots of virtue sown by the buddhas, bodhisattvas, pratyekabuddhas, and śrāvakas throughout all time, while feeling glad when your enemies suffer, is to wrongly understand rejoicing.

We wrongly understand patience if we are unable to tolerate difficulties with respect to our Dharma practice but are able to, on the other hand, bear all sorts of difficulties to accomplish worldly goals.

We wrongly understand aspiration if we have no aspiration to practice Dharma but have a lot of energy for the pursuit of worldly goals, such as getting food, clothing, and so on.

We wrongly understand savoring if we prefer to savor the worldly happiness produced by attachment, hatred, and ignorance instead of savoring the work of listening to, thinking about, and meditating on Dharma.

We wrongly understand compassion if we do not feel compassion for sentient beings suffering in the three lower realms but are unhappy when we see religious people who do not have quite enough food, clothing, and so on.

We wrongly understand what a caring attitude is if we influence other people to misuse the property of a spiritual community and lead them to act wrongly, instead of inducing them to observe the Dharma and encouraging them in such good deeds as listening to, thinking about, and meditating on Dharma.

We wrongly understand rejoicing if we feel happy when others encounter problems and suffering, instead of rejoicing in the virtues of buddhas, bodhisattvas, pratyekabuddhas, and śrāvakas.

Don't be sporadic.

You should not sometimes train your mind and not train it at others. Instead, single-pointedly and continuously train your mind, this being the great way followed by all buddhas throughout time.

We shouldn't practice training the mind with exaggerated effort for a while and then later cease practicing for a period, when tired or discouraged. It is vital that we train our minds steadily and continuously with a consistent amount of energy and effort.

Train with decisiveness.

Resolve to train your mind continually by completely surrendering your mind to the mind training itself. Having resolved to do so, train your mind.

Free yourself with the duo of investigation and analysis.

Make an effort to investigate which afflictions are more gross and flagrant in your heart. Then having precisely analyzed, with a righteous motivation, the referents, causes, and such that produce those afflictions, work at the means to not produce them.

We should constantly examine whether afflictions appear in our hearts. If we find that a certain affliction is there, we should immediately try to eradicate it by administering the appropriate antidote.

Don't boast.

Do not boast of your lengthy practice of Dharma, your learnedness, uprightness, and so on, nor brag about the insignificant ways in which you have benefited others. Instead, act in accordance with what Dromtön Rinpoche taught: "Pray to the deity without any expectation of humans."

We should never feel superior or special and consequently boast to others of our spiritual progress as a result of training our minds. Rather, we should find ourselves becoming more and more humble and increasingly able to see ourselves as lower than others. So we should never boast of having done something beneficial for others, nor should we remind others of what we have done for them in hopes that they will feel obliged to help us in return. Instead, as Dromtönpa said, we should not have any expectations regarding humans, and we should rely on and have faith in the Three Jewels.

Don't be bad tempered.

If you make a big deal out of things that are of little importance—the disparaging remarks or insults of others, little improprieties in their way of speaking to you, their way of looking at you, or their way of acting toward you, whether right or wrong—you won't be able to bear your own suffering and illness. By meaninglessly ruminating, day and night, on what happened until there is no room in your mind for anything else, you develop a bad temper. As this will bring you to ruin, don't ever develop such an attitude.

We should never resentfully hold a grudge against others when they insult or disparage us, look at us with unpleasant expressions, or speak badly to us. We should always keep a relaxed state of mind.

Don't be fickle.

Do not exhibit a demeanor of liking and disliking trifling things. Such behavior would thoroughly annoy your companions.

We should be careful not to always be having sudden swings in our emotions, such as being instantly pleased and happy when some small pleasant thing happens and, on the other hand, being immediately angry and unhappy when some trivial unpleasantness occurs. Instead, if we are training the mind we must do away with such fickle and moody behavior and keep our minds under control in all situations.

Don't wish for gratitude.

Practice Dharma without hoping that someone will thank you for it or acknowledge the good you have done for others. Practice without hoping that you will thereby gain a good reputation, either.

We should not take up training our minds for the purpose of achieving happiness in our future lives or to achieve worldly happiness, such as gratitude, a good reputation, offerings, and so forth, in this life. Instead, we should practice training our minds in a meaningful and positive way, such that it is true Dharma practice and a cause for enlightenment.

COLOPHON

Geshe Chekawa's Colophon

Geshe Chekawa, who had gained confidence in the enlightened attitude of bodhicitta, said:

> Disregarding suffering and slander
> I sought out instruction in taming selfishness
> because of my many aspirations.
> Now I have no regrets even when I die.

The Kadam geshe, Chekawa, who fully integrated and developed stability in the practice of training the mind, composed this text known as *Seven Steps for Training the Mind*.

Gomo Tulku's Colophon

These instructions, the quintessence of nectar, greatly benefit the hearts of everyone, including myself. This is because we cannot become a buddha just by meditating on emptiness without being instructed in training in the enlightened attitude of bodhicitta. The enlightened attitude is in fact the defining characteristic of the

Mahāyāna. This is why bodhicitta is praised hundreds of times across the many Mahāyāna sutras and treatises. Glorious Candrakīrti, for example, says to see compassion alone as the seed of a spiritual victor's perfect harvest.

I, who am called Gomo Tulku, having borrowed some mind training texts, wrote this memorandum in Dharamsala, India in 1962. I wrote, greatly celebrating these texts from the depths of my heart, mainly to perpetually remind myself of the practice of training the mind. As I wrote, I prayed, "How wonderful it would be if this text were to cause each and every one of my former mother sentient beings scattered throughout space to practice such a path."

As a result of having written it, may the precious teachings of the Victor spread, flourish, and remain forever, and may the holy ones who uphold the teachings live long, the lotuses at their feet planted firmly for hundreds of eons. May my having written this text cause me and all sentient beings scattered throughout space, my mothers of old, to quickly develop in our hearts the precious enlightened attitude of bodhicitta, to thereafter realize thusness and complete the two stages of the tantric path. May we thereby easily attain unsurpassable great enlightenment, the precious state of union.

These instructions on training the mind, the quintessence of all the teachings of the Buddha, are of great benefit to the hearts of sentient beings. This is because we cannot attain buddhahood simply by realizing emptiness without developing the enlightened attitude of bodhicitta. In addition, whether or not what we practice is actually Mahāyāna depends entirely on whether we have developed the enlightened attitude of bodhicitta.

Given the importance and preciousness of bodhicitta, scholars very often praise it. Candrakīrti, for example, wrote in *Entering the Middle Way*:

> Compassion should be thought of as like the seed
>   for the massive harvest of spiritual victors, like
>   water for its growth,
> and like its fruit which gives long-lasting
>   enjoyment—thus do I praise compassion first
>   and foremost.

In fact, the great commentators on both sutra and tantra often praise the enlightened attitude of bodhicitta. Because I too so deeply admire the enlightened attitude, I extensively studied the mind training texts and wrote this commentary on them to remind myself of the practice. I also prayed that this commentary would benefit many other sentient beings and dedicated any virtue amassed by composing this text toward the long life of all the holy ones who preserve the Buddha's teachings, toward the flourishing of the Buddha's teachings, and toward the swift development of the enlightened attitude and attainment of buddhahood on the part of all sentient beings. You too should similarly dedicate the virtue you have earned by reading about and studying the practice of training the mind.

APPENDIX: TIBETAN TEXT

།།ཐེག་པ་ཆེན་པོའི་བློ་སྦྱོང་དོན་བདུན་མའི་རྩ་བ།།

ཕྱགས་རྗེ་ཆེན་པོ་ལ་ཕྱག་འཚལ་ལོ།

།མན་ངག་བདུད་རྩིའི་སྙིང་པོ་འདི། །གསེར་གྱིང་པ་ནས་བརྒྱུད་པ་ཡིན།
།རྡོ་རྗེ་ཉི་མ་སྟོན་ཤིང་བཞིན། །གཞུང་དོན་ལ་སོགས་ཤེས་པར་བྱ།
།སྐྱིགས་མ་ལྔ་པོ་བདོ་བ་འདི། །བྱང་ཆུབ་ལམ་དུ་བསྒྱུར་བ་ཡིན།

།)

།དང་པོ་སྔོན་འགྲོ་དག་ལ་བསླབ།

།༢

།ལས་ལན་ཐམས་ཅད་གཅིག་ལ་བདའ།

།ཀུན་ལ་བཀའ་དྲིན་ཆེ་བར་བསྒོམ།

།གཏོང་ལེན་གཉིས་པོ་སྤེལ་མར་སྦྱང་།

།ལེན་པའི་གོ་རིམ་རང་ནས་བརྩམ།

།དེ་གཉིས་རླུང་ལ་བསྐྱོན་པར་བྱ།

།ཡུལ་གསུམ་དུག་གསུམ་དགེ་རྩ་གསུམ།

།རྗེས་ཀྱི་མན་ངག་མདོར་བསྡུས་པ།

།དེ་ལ་དྲན་པས་བསྐུལ་བའི་ཕྱིར།

།སྤྱོད་ལམ་ཀུན་ཏུ་ཚིག་གིས་སྦྱང་།

།བཏུན་པ་ཐོབ་ནས་གསང་བ་བསྟན།

།ཆོས་རྣམས་རྨི་ལམ་ལྟ་བུར་བསམ།

།མ་སྐྱེས་རིག་པའི་གཞིས་ལ་དཔྱད།

།གཉེན་པོ་ཉིད་ཀྱང་རང་སར་གྲོལ།

།ལམ་གྱི་ངོ་བོ་ཀུན་གཞིའི་ངང་དུ་བཞག

།ཐུན་མཚམས་སྒྱུ་མའི་སྐྱེས་བུར་བྱ།

༣

།སྤྱོད་བཅུད་ཕྱིག་པས་གདང་བའི་ཚེས། །ཀྱེན་ངན་བྱང་ཆུབ་ལམ་དུ་བསྒྱུར།

།འཕྲལ་ལ་གང་ཐུག་བསྒོམ་དུ་སྦྱར། །སྤྱོར་བ་བཞི་ལྡན་ཐབས་ཀྱི་མཆོག

༩

།མན་ངག་སྙིང་པོ་མདོར་བསྡུས་པ། །སྟོབས་ལྔ་དག་དང་བསྒྱུར་བར་བྱ།
།ཐེག་ཆེན་འཕོ་བའི་གདམས་ངག་ནི། །སྟོབས་ལྔ་ཉིད་ཡིན་སྐྱོང་ལམ་གཅེས།

༥

།ཆོས་ཀུན་དགོངས་པ་གཅིག་ཏུ་འདུས།
།དཔང་པོ་གཉིས་ཀྱི་གཙོ་བོ་བཟུང་།
།ཡིད་བདེ་འབའ་ཞིག་རྒྱུན་དུ་བསྟེན།
།ཡེངས་བའི་ཆད་ནེ་ལོག་པ་མིན།
།འདིུངས་རྟགས་ཆེན་པོ་ལྷ་ལྷུན་ཡིན།
།ཡིངས་ཀྱང་ཐུབ་ན་འདྲོགས་པ་ཡིན།

༦

།སྒྲི་དོན་གསུམ་ལ་རྟག་ཏུ་བསླབ།
།འདུན་པ་བསྒྱུར་ལ་རང་སོར་བཞག
།ཡན་ལག་ཉམས་པ་བརྟེན་མི་བྱ།
།གཞན་ཕྱོགས་གང་ཡང་མི་བསམ་མོ།
།ཉིན་མོངས་གང་ཆེ་སྔོན་ལ་སྦྱང་།

།འབྲས་བུ་རེ་བ་ཐམས་ཅད་སྤང་།

།དུག་ཅན་གྱི་ཟས་སྤང་།

།གཞུང་བཟང་པོ་མི་བསྟེན།

།ཁགས་ངན་མ་རྐོད།

།འཕྱང་མ་སྒྲུག

།གནད་ལ་མི་དབབ།

།མཛོ་ཁལ་གླང་ལ་མི་བྱ།

།མགྱོགས་ཀྱི་རྩེ་མི་གཏོད།

།གཏོ་ལོག་མི་བྱ།

།ལྷ་བདུད་དུ་མི་དབབ།

།སྐྱིད་ཀྱི་ཡན་ལག་ཏུ་སྡུག་མ་ཚོལ།

ༀ

།རྣལ་འབྱོར་ཐམས་ཅད་གཅིག་གིས་བྱ།

།ལོག་གནོན་ཐམས་ཅད་གཅིག་གིས་བྱ།

།ཐོག་མཐའ་གཉིས་ལ་བྱ་བ་གཉིས།

།གཉིས་པོ་གང་བྱུང་བཟོད་པར་བྱ།

།གཉིས་པོ་སྲོག་དང་བསྡོས་ལ་བསྲུང་།

།དགའ་བ་གསུམ་ལ་བསྒྲུབ་པར་བྱ།

།ཀྲུ་ཡི་གཙོ་བོ་རྣམ་གསུམ་བླང་།

།ཉམས་པ་མེད་པ་རྣམ་གསུམ་བསྟེན།

།འབྲལ་མེད་གསུམ་དང་ལྡན་པར་བྱ།

།ཡུལ་ལ་ཕྱོགས་མེད་དག་ཏུ་སྤྱོང་།

།ཁྱབ་དང་གཏིང་འབྱོངས་ཀུན་ལ་གཅེས།

།བཀོལ་བ་རྣམས་ལ་ཐུག་ཏུ་བསྐྱོམ།

།ཀྲེན་གཞན་དག་ལ་སྟེས་མི་བྱ།

།ད་རེས་གཙོ་བོ་ཉམས་སུ་བླང་།

།གོ་ལོག་མི་བྱ།

།རེས་འཇོག་མི་བྱ།

།དོལ་ཆོད་དུ་སྒྲུང་།

།བཏག་དཔྱད་གཉིས་ཀྱིས་ཐར་བར་བྱ།

།ཡུས་མ་བསྐྱོམ།

།གོ་ལོང་མ་སྟོམ།

།ཡུད་ཙམ་པ་མི་བྱ།

།ཛིར་ཆེ་མ་འདོད།

།།རང་གི་མོས་པ་མཐང་པོའི་རྒྱུས། །སྔག་བསྒྲལ་གཏུམ་ངན་ཁྱད་བསད་ནས།

།བདག་འཛིན་འདུལ་བའི་གདམས་ངག་ཞུས། །ད་ནི་ཤི་ཡང་མི་འགྱོད་དོ།།

NOTES

1. These three—ethical discipline, meditative concentration, and wisdom—are the three trainings that constitute the true path. There are three aspects to a bodhisattva's ethical discipline: the ethical conduct of restraint, the ethical conduct of practicing virtue to create the merit to attain enlightenment, and the ethical discipline of actively helping others by taking action with one's body, speech, and mind. Meditative concentration refers specifically to the mind remaining single-pointedly without distraction, unmixed with the stains of the mental afflictions, but it is also a general term encompassing a wide variety of meditation practices and levels of concentration. Wisdom refers to the realization of the final nature of all phenomena; it is direct comprehension of emptiness, the lack of inherent existence of self and phenomena.

2. Enlightenment is the ultimate goal of Mahayana Buddhist practice, attained when all limitations have been removed from the mind and all one's positive potential has been realized. It is a state characterized by unlimited compassion, power, and wisdom.

3. Langri Thangpa Dorje Sengé (Glang ri thang pa rdo rje seng ge), "Eight Verses for Training the Mind" (*blo sbyong tshig rkang brgyad ma*), in *Blo sbyong brgya rtsa dang dkar chag gdung sel zla ba bcas*, compiled by Dkon mchog rgyal mtshan (Dharamsala: Shes rig par khang, 1973.)

4. For more information on the origins of the mind training texts see Thupten Jinpa's *Mind Training: The Great Collection* (Boston: Wisdom, 2006).

5. The preliminary meditations are found in a genre of Tibetan Buddhist texts called stages of the path, or *lamrim* in Tibetan, the origins of which are attributed to a well-known text also by Atiśa, *Lamp for*

the Path to Enlightenment (Bodhipathapradīpa). This particular way of compiling the Buddha's teachings in an accessible and structured format aimed at making them easy to practice (or at least easier!) was later widely promulgated in Tibet by Tsongkhapa Losang Drakpa (1357–1419), particularly in his magnum opus *The Great Treatise on the Stages of the Path to Enlightenment*.

6. Samsara is often misunderstood to refer to the worlds inhabited by sentient beings. It is marked by suffering, impermanence, and a mistaken sense of self characterized by rebirth in one or another unsatisfactory realm due to the force of actions and affliction.

7. The mental afflictions are a class of dissonant mental states, including both thoughts and emotions, that have their root in ignorance. They are referred to as "afflictions" because they afflict the individual from deep within. The classical Buddhist texts on psychology list six root afflictions—(1) attachment, (2) aversion, (3) pride, (4) afflicted doubt, (5) ignorance, and (6) afflicted view—and twenty afflictions that are derivative of these root afflictions.

8. In the context of the practice of training the mind, "sense of self" and "self-importance" have very precise meanings. "Sense of self" (*bdag 'dzin*) refers to instinctively believing in the intrinsic existence of your own self. "Self" here means a substantial, truly existing "I" or "me." The wisdom that realizes emptiness eliminates this mistaken notion of self. "Self-importance" or "self-centeredness" (*bdag gces*) refers to the deeply ingrained attitude that cherishes the welfare of your own self above all others and makes you oblivious to others' well-being. These are the "twin demons" that lie within our hearts and serve as the source of all misfortune and downfall. These two thoughts—a mistaken sense of self and a sense of self-importance—are the primary focus of combat in the practice of training the mind.

9. *bdag nyid gces 'dzin sdug bsngal kun gyi rgyu | gzhan rnams gces 'dzin phun tshogs kun gyi gzhi |*

10. "Foundational Verses for Training the Mind" (*Blo sbyong rtsa tshig*), in *Collected Works of Keutsang Jamyang Monlam (Ke'u tshang sprul sku blo bzang jam dbyangs smon lam gyi gsung 'bum)* (Dharamsala: Library of Tibetan Works and Archives, 1984.)

11. In Mahāyāna Buddhism, "nonabiding nirvana" is the nirvana attained by a buddha, who abides neither in the tumult of samsara nor the quietistic peace of final nirvana. It signifies that in Mahāyāna,

enlightened beings remain active in the world, though they are not "of it."

12. Emptiness is the central theme in Mahāyāna philosophy and the truth that must be realized if enlightenment is to be attained. A radicalization and universalization of the early Buddhist idea of no-self, emptiness is the true nature of all entities and concepts in both samsara and nirvana, variously taken to be the absence of inherent existence or external objects' nondifference from the mind that perceives them.

13. Wisdom can refer simply to intelligence or mental aptitude, but here, in the context of the Mahāyāna path, wisdom refers to the wisdom aspect of the path constituted primarily by deep insight into the emptiness of all things.

14. Method refers to the altruistic deeds of the bodhisattva, including the cultivation of compassion and the enlightened attitude of bodhicitta. In Mahāyāna Buddhism, the union of method and wisdom is central to understanding the path.

15. Śrāvakas are disciples of the Buddha whose primary spiritual objective is to attain liberation from the cycle of existence. Śrāvakas are often paired with *pratyekabuddha*s, who seek liberation on the basis of autonomous practice as opposed to listening to others' instructions. An *arhat* is any being who has eliminated all afflictions in themselves, completed the path, and attained nirvana. According to most Mahayanists, arhatship, while tranquil, is a goal inferior to the full buddhahood altruistically sought by the bodhisattva, and arhats eventually will have to move beyond the limitations of their quiescent state.

16. Traditional Tibetan medical texts enumerate 404 types of illness. With regard to them, *Mirror of Beryl* states: "These illnesses have been classified as fourfold: 101 ailments that disappear by themselves and need no treatment, 101 illnesses caused by spirits that are cured when treated, 101 illnesses that are cured if treated but not if left untreated, and 101 illnesses that even treatment cannot cure."

17. "These texts" refers to "the six texts of the Kadam": *Ornament for the Mahāyāna Sutras* (*Mahāyānasūtrālaṁkāra*), *The Bodhisattva Levels* (*Bodhisattvabhūmi*), *Guide to the Bodhisattva's Way of Life* (*Bodhisattvacaryāvatāra*), *Compendium of Training* (*Śikṣāsamucchaya*), *Buddha's Life Stories* (*Jātakamāla*), and *Indicative Verses* (*Udānavarga*).

18. The physical form in which the enlightened mind appears in order to benefit ordinary beings.
19. Abhisamayālaṁkāra 8:33.

    *karoti yena citrāṇi hitāni jagataḥ samaṃ | ābhavāt so
    'nupacchinnaḥ kāyo nairmāṇiko muneḥ ||
    gang gis srid pa ji srid par 'gro la phan pa sna tshogs dag |
    mnyam du mdzad pa'i sku de ni thub pa'i sprul sku rgyun
    mi 'chad ||*

20. Abhisamayālaṁkāra 8: 34a.

    *tathā karmāpy anucchinnam asyā saṃsāram iṣyate |
    de bzhin 'khor ba ji srid 'di'i las ni rgyun mi 'chad par 'dod |*

21. See Tsong-Kha-Pa, *The Great Treatise on the Stages of the Path to Enlightenment, Volume 1* (Ithaca: Snow Lion, 2000), pp. 85–86.
22. See Geshe Rabten, *The Essential Nectar: Meditations on the Buddhist Path*, (Boston: Wisdom, 2014), pp. 73–74.
23. Stages of the path or *lamrim* is a genre of instruction on the Mahāyāna Buddhist path that evolved from Atiśa's *Lamp for the Path to Enlightenment*. This short text lays out the essence of the entire teachings of the Buddha within a graduated framework of practices that are geared to three levels of mental capability. Tsongkhapa's *Great Treatise on the Stages of the Path* is the most well known of the later Tibetan works inspired by Atiśa's text.
24. The six drawbacks general to existence are:
    1. things are uncertain
    2. thirst for sensual pleasure is insatiable
    3. we repeatedly lose our lives
    4. we have to be repeatedly born again
    5. we constantly fluctuate between high and low states
    6. we have no companions
25. The threefold suffering general to existence is:
    1. suffering of suffering
    2. suffering of change
    3. suffering of conditionality
26. It is a common Tibetan belief that the hooting of an owl at night augurs misfortune.
27. The Tibetan term *tonglen* literally means "giving and taking," with "giving" occupying the first position in the sequence. However, the term has been translated in this book as "taking and giving" in accor-

dance with the order in which the two are usually practiced—that is, taking followed by giving.

28. This is literally the "mind-only" school of Mahāyāna philosophy, which defines the crucial concept of emptiness in terms of either an object's lack of difference from the subject perceiving it, or dependent phenomena's lack of the imaginary nature that has been imputed to them. The Cittamātra School of philosophy specifically proposes a seventh and eighth types of consciousness in addition to the six consciousnesses (the consciousnesses of the five senses and of the mental sense) accepted by all Buddhists—namely, an afflicted mental consciousness and a basis-of-all consciousness.

29. The philosophical viewpoint arrived at by the Prasaṅgika Madhyamaka School is considered within Tibetan Buddhist traditions to be the pinnacle of Buddhist thought and to represent the final view of Śākyamuni Buddha himself.

30. In ancient India magicians and illusionists were thought to work by using spell-like mantras or magical salves on their audiences in order to effect the illusion of one thing, such as a stick or pebble, appearing as another.

31. Observance of the ten virtues forms the heart of Buddhist ethical discipline. Since ethical discipline is conceived in terms of refraining from harmful behavior, the ten virtues are negatively phrased, reflecting the avoidance of ten nonvirtuous behaviors:

    1. not killing
    2. not stealing
    3. not engaging in sexual misconduct
    4. not lying
    5. not slandering
    6. not speaking harshly
    7. not speaking senselessly
    8. not being covetous
    9. not being malicious
    10. not holding wrong views

32. In Tibetan culture, ritual cakes are used as offerings for protective spirits or tutelary deities. The cakes are typically made from an unbaked dough of toasted barley flour and water and are conical in shape.

33. Deities that protect or guard the teachings of the Buddha and its followers.

34. The ritual of one hundred offering cakes is a specific Tibetan practice of offering the Dharma protectors many small round ritual cakes. The burnt flour ritual is a ritual in which a burnt offering of toasted barley flour mixed with butter and six excellent substances—nutmeg, saffron, cloves, black cardamom, green cardamom, and bamboo marrow—is offered to the Dharma protectors.

35. The five actions of immediate retribution are deeds of such a heinous nature that the perpetrator will depart after death to the lowest form of existence with no break at all. The five are:
    1. killing one's father
    2. killing one's mother
    3. killing an arhat
    4. wounding the body of a buddha
    5. creating a schism within the monastic community

36. The two accumulations are the masses of merit and wisdom that one builds up as one practices the path. "Merit" refers to the stored up acts of virtuous karma that one engages in and "wisdom" refers specifically to a realization of the nature of things that is profound and liberating. The qualities of the Buddha's physical body are attained as a result of building up the accumulation of merit, and the qualities of his mind are attained as a result of building up the accumulation of wisdom.

37. The seven-part prayer is composed of seven aspects of ritual offering that are crucial to meditation in Mahāyāna Buddhism:
    1. prostration
    2. offering
    3. confession
    4. rejoicing in the virtue of oneself and others
    5. requesting the buddhas to turn the Dharma wheel, that is, to teach the Dharma
    6. entreating them not to enter final nirvana
    7. dedication of merit

38. "The intermediate state" refers to the period, no longer than forty-nine days, that occurs between death and a subsequent rebirth. During this period, mourning rituals are conducted, and the liberation of the mind still may be effected.

39. "Transferring consciousness" refers to the process of forcibly separating the consciousness, or primordial body, from the coarse body in order to take another life without going through the death and

intermediate-state process. It also refers to the more commonly known practice of ensuring, with a lama's help, migration into a pure land at the time of death.

40. In tantric theory, the related physical and mental energies or "winds" that course through the subtle body are the true basis for what sentient beings are and become. In its subtlest form, the wind-mind is found in the indestructible drop at the heart chakra.

41. The ten acts of Mahāyāna Dharma may refer to "the ten perfections":
    1. generosity
    2. ethical discipline
    3. patience
    4. joyous effort
    5. meditative concentration
    6. wisdom
    7. skillful means
    8. prayer
    9. power
    10. exalted wisdom

    Or they may refer to the various religious acts of:
    1. copying down scriptures
    2. making offerings
    3. giving gifts
    4. listening to Dharma
    5. upholding Dharma
    6. reading Dharma
    7. explaining Dharma
    8. reciting Dharma
    9. thinking about the meaning of Dharma
    10. meditating on the meaning of Dharma

42. The factors contributing to the enlightened attitude of bodhicitta are great compassion, love, and so on.

43. Cultivation of the sevenfold cause and effect is one of the techniques used to develop bodhicitta. One cultivates six mindsets that act as the causes that give rise to the singular result of bodhicitta. The six mindsets one cultivates are:
    1. to recognize that all sentient beings have been our mothers in previous lives
    2. to remember their great kindness during those times

3. to wish to repay their kindness
4. to give rise to a feeling of love for them
5. to develop a sense of compassion for them
6. to develop a special determination to take responsibility for securing the happiness of all living beings and for eliminating their suffering

These mindsets, when cultivated together, produce as their singular effect the altruistic enlightened attitude of bodhicitta itself. This technique is spelled out in greater detail in Phabongkha Rinpoche's *Liberation in the Palm of Your Hands*.

44. In Tibetan culture spirits that reside in or near rocks, trees, water, and other such areas are thought to cause diseases when disturbed.

45. The bodhisattva vows are a special set of vows to observe restraint with regard to behavior that harms others. The eighteen root vows entail avoiding all of the following actions:

1. praising oneself and belittling others
2. not sharing material or spiritual wealth
3. not accepting apologies or striking others
4. giving up Mahāyāna and teaching something one has made up
5. taking offerings intended for the Three Jewels
6. giving up the Dharma
7. causing the ordained to disrobe
8. committing any of the five acts of immediate retribution
9. holding an antagonistic outlook
10. destroying towns or places where people live
11. teaching emptiness to those who are not ready to hear it
12. causing others to turn away from enlightenment
13. causing others to give up their personal vows
14. belittling Buddhists who do not practice Mahāyāna
15. proclaiming false realization of emptiness
16. accepting things that have been stolen from the Three Jewels
17. establishing unfair policies
18. giving up on bodhicitta

The forty-six secondary bodhisattva vows deal with avoiding specific faulty behavior that impairs our training in the six perfections: seven faulty acts that hinder training in the perfection of generosity (1–7), nine faulty acts that hinder training in the perfection of ethical discipline (8–16), four faulty acts that hinder training in the perfection of patience (17–20), three faulty acts that hinder training in the perfection of joyous effort (21–23), three faulty acts that hinder training in the perfection of meditative concentration (23–26), eight faulty acts that hinder training in the perfection of wisdom (27–34), and twelve faulty acts that contradict working for the benefit of others (35–46).

46. In the original Tibetan, this line of the text refers to a *dzo* and a *lang*, two animals the distinct size and load-bearing capacity of which most Tibetans would be very familiar with. A *dzo* is a cross between a yak and a *lang*, or domestic cow. It is reputed to be much stronger than a cow. To render the aphorism more readily transparent to English readers, we have replaced *dzo* and *lang* with "horse" and "pony," two animals the size and load-bearing capacity of which most English readers will be readily familiar with.

47. The vows of personal liberation, the bodhisattva vows, and the tantric vows are the three types of vows used in Buddhism. The vows of personal liberation are the code of disciplined behavior elaborated in the Vinaya portion of Buddhist canons. They are divided into eight types: vows for monks, nuns, novice monks, novice nuns, probationary renunciates, laymen, laywomen, and one-day vow-holders. The bodhisattva vows are those vows peculiar to practitioners of the Mahāyāna. See note 45 for further details. The tantric vows are those vows taken in association with initiation into the practice of tantra. A practicing Buddhist may hold one set of vows, multiple sets, or only take vows periodically on special occasions.

48. This line and its commentary are missing in Gomo Rinpoche's text. They were translated from the Italian and inserted here by the English translator. The precise source of these lines is unknown.

A BRIEF BIOGRAPHY
OF GOMO TULKU

GOMO TULKU (1922–1985) was the twenty-second incarnation of Sonam Rinchen, a highly realized Tibetan yogi who was one of the main disciples of the Indian mahasiddha Padampa Sanggye, a contemporary of the well-known Tibetan saint Milarepa (1052–1135). Gomo is the name of a mountainous locality in the Penpo region of central Tibet associated with the deity Chakrasamvara. Here Padampa Sanggye once lived and taught, and here his direct disciple Sonam Rinchen founded Gomo Hermitage with more than a hundred monks and a hundred meditators, and a nunnery of about seventy nuns. Among his disciples were many who attained enlightenment in that very lifetime. On his passing away, Sonam Rinchen's body was not cremated but placed inside a stupa within the monastery grounds where it remained without decomposing until its destruction by the Chinese.

Many of Sonam Rinchen's subsequent incarnations manifested as highly realized beings and qualified practitioners of Vajrayogini. When the twenty-first incarnation, who was recognized when he was already quite old, passed away, the administrators of Penpo Ganden Chökor

Monastery requested Kyabje Pabongka Dechen Nyingpo to help them find his incarnation. This master identified the twenty-second incarnation of Sonam Rinchen to be a young child born in Penpo in the third month of the water-dog year (1922) to a family named Penpo Chang-rasar. This family, who belonged to the nobility, worked for the government and were also quite wealthy farmers. Following his official recognition as the incarnation of Sonam Rinchen, the young boy was escorted by a great procession to his monastery, Penpo Ganden Chökor, where he was received with great ceremony. A short time later, the Thirteenth Dalai Lama also confirmed that the five-year-old child was indeed the incarnation of Sonam Rinchen.

At his monastery in Penpo, the young incarnate lama, known as Gomo Tulku, studied the alphabet, reading, and writing, and memorized many of the monastery's prayers and rituals. From the ages of nine to eleven, he studied at the mountain hermitage of Pabongka Dechen Nyingpo, Trashi Chöling, where he received many initiations, transmissions, and oral instructions from Pabongka Rinpoche himself. Gomo Tulku then entered Sera Je Monastery where he studied the great treatises with Geshe Ngawang Jinpa.

During his years at Sera and regular visits to his own monastery, Gomo Tulku memorized many tantric texts, received numerous initiations, and did many retreats. At the age of twenty, he received full ordination from Yong-dzin Purchog Rinpoche (Purbuchog) and, at the age of twenty-five, completed the degree of Geshe Lingsel. He subsequently entered the Lower Tantric College where he studied and memorized the rituals of the deities associated with the four classes of tantra.

At the age of twenty-six, Gomo Tulku left the monastic life and married; however, he remained at Ganden Chökor Monastery in his position as head lama and continued to teach and confer initiations. At the beginning of the Chinese invasion of Tibet, Gomo Tulku, age thirty-six, departed for India with his wife and one-year-old daughter, Pema Yangkey. From 1960 to 1962, he served as the principal of the Tibetan school in Madras (now known as Chennai), during which time his second daughter, Yanki Chöden, was born. Gomo Tulku together with his family then moved north to Mussorie where for the next twenty-two years he served as the foster father of a children's home. For eighteen years, from 1964 onward, on the full moon of the fourth Tibetan month of Saka Dawa, Rinpoche organized and led an annual fasting retreat (*nyung-ne*) in which more than a hundred people regularly participated. He also introduced a yearly recitation of 100 million *om mani padme hum* mantras and oversaw the construction of a large prayer wheel containing more than 1.4 billion *mani* mantras housed in a building with walls lined with statues of the thousand buddhas of this fortunate eon.

Gomo Tulku received initiations principally from Kyabje Pabongka Rinpoche and Taggyab Rinpoche. In addition, he received initiations, teachings, and the transmissions of texts from His Holiness the Fourteenth Dalai Lama, Ling Rinpoche, and Trijang Rinpoche, as well as from many other highly qualified teachers. Being the holder of many rare lineages of initiations, transmissions, and teachings, several of Gomo Tulku's gurus advised him to take particular care to preserve these lineages by passing them on to others. Aware of this, Lama Thubten Yeshe, spiritual founder of the Foundation for the Preservation of the Mahayana Tradition (FPMT), requested Gomo Tulku to pass on the rare lineages of initiations and transmissions to his Western disciples. Later, when he was very sick in Delhi, Lama Yeshe asked Lama Thubten Zopa Rinpoche to repeat this request. As a result, Gomo Tulku arrived at Istituto Lama Tzong Khapa, Pomaia, Italy, at the beginning of January 1985. He subsequently taught at three Italian FPMT centers for a total of three and a half months, conferring entire collections of initiations, the transmission of the *Eight Thousand Stanza Perfection of Wisdom Sutra*, and tantric commentaries. In addition, he gave teachings on the stages of the path (*lamrim*) and mind training (*lojong*) and taught ritual dancing, chanting, and torma making. During this time, many students, impressed by his tireless energy for teaching and his ability to inspire others to practice Dharma, became very devoted to him.

Gomo Tulku then spent a month and a half teaching and conferring initiations in FPMT centers in France, Spain, and Germany. At the end of May 1985, having concluded his European tour, Rinpoche unexpectedly decided to return to his family in India, canceling his scheduled teaching tour in Australia. Soon after his return to India, he was diagnosed with advanced liver cancer and on the fifteenth day of the sixth month of the Tibetan calendar (July 31, 1985) Gomo Tulku passed away. Disciples present at his death testified that rainbows appeared in the sky and that his body did not begin to decay, nor did it even change color, for three days, but remained sitting upright in the meditation posture. Following his cremation, people saw an image of the Buddha in the ashes and the footprint of a small child pointing north.

Signs during his lifetime also attested to Gomo Tulku's spiritual achievements; for example, on several occasions when Rinpoche was conferring initiations, rainbows and other auspicious signs were seen by those present. When the Fourteenth Dalai Lama first traveled to central Tibet from Amdo as a young child, he visited Gomo Tulku at his monastery. This was during the time of the autumn rains, and Gomo Rinpoche, having been asked to stop the heavy rain, did so for an entire week. Later on at the age of twenty-seven, while he was giving the transmission of the Kangyur to a large number of people, there was the threat of very heavy snowfall. Gomo Tulku was requested to prevent a possible calamity and complied by blessing hundreds of sacks of rock-salt that were then burned continually for several days over evergreen branches in a circular trench. The heavy snow did not fall. Also during Rinpoche's stay at Istituto Lama Tzong Khapa in the winter of 1985 unusual heavy snow fell and temperatures dropped below freezing, resulting in a loss of electricity and frozen water pipes. Rinpoche, having been requested to stop the snow, blessed some rock-salt that was then burned in the courtyard; soon after, a distinct circle of clear sky appeared above the Institute.

The twenty-third incarnation of Sonam Rinchen, Tenzin D. Kashhi, was born August 8, 1988, in Montreal, Canada, to Yanki Chödrön, the youngest daughter of Gomo Tulku. Officially recognized by His Holiness the Fourteenth Dalai Lama, he was enthroned at the age of seven by Lama Zopa Rinpoche at Istituto Lama Tzong Khapa, Pomaia, Italy, on September 7, 1995, and once again at Sera Jey Monastery in South India on July 14, 1996. Like other young reincarnate lamas, Gomo Tulku, who received the ordination name of Tenzin Lhundrub Sangpo from His Holiness the Fourteenth Dalai Lama, followed a traditional monastic education to prepare him for his role as a recognized incarnate lama. At the age of eighteen, he successfully completed the first twelve years of philosophical studies in a ceremony of public debate (Rigchung) before thousands of monk scholars. Soon after Gomo Tulku decided to leave the monastic life to pursue his interest in music. He is dedicated to developing and supporting ventures that will help the Tibetan community, both inside and outside Tibet.

INDEX

A

absolute enlightened attitude, 49–52
  being an illusionist, 52–53, n30
  defined, 3
  examining the nature of unborn awareness, 50
  focusing on the basis of all (emptiness), 51–52
  learning the secret of emptiness, 49
  never straying from, 105
  phenomena are not truly existent, 51
  regarding phenomena as dreamlike, 49–50
  unifying with relative bodhicitta, 49
  See also bodhicitta
accumulations, two, 68, n36
actions
  beginning and ending each day, 100–101
  devotion to guru in, 33
  doing single-mindedly, 99
  of immediate retribution, five, 60, n35

  preliminary meditation on, 38
  ten acts of Mahāyāna Dharma, 83, 84, n41
  virtuous, never straying from, 105–6
adversity, using, 55–65
  applying circumstances to meditation, 57
  four practices for, 58–64
  for mind training, 11, 81–82
  for self-transformation, 11
  text on, 14
  transforming conditions, 26, 55–56, 85–86, 99–100
ambush, not lying in, 94–95
anger, special cases regarding, 107–8
Annotations to Foundational Verses for Training the Mind, 11
antidotes, 58, 62–63, 68, 72
arhatship, 22, n15
around-the-clock practice, 9
ascetic, great, 83, 84
Atiśa, 4, 20, 23–24, 30, n5, n23

B

bad temper, 112–13

ABOUT THE TRANSLATOR

 JOAN NICELL first met the Buddhist teachings and meditation practice while traveling in Thailand in 1986. A year later she met her main teacher, Lama Thubten Zopa Rinpoche, and soon afterward attended her first course in the Tibetan Buddhist tradition. She was ordained as a nun by His Holiness the Dalai Lama in Dharamsala in 1989. From 1990 to 2012 she lived at Lama Tzong Khapa Institute in Pomaia, Italy. Here she translated texts for the residential and online study programs as well as for weekend courses and retreats, transcribed the teachings of the Basic Program and Masters Program, and was responsible for implementing and running these two in depth programs. She presently coordinates the foundation level Buddhist programs for FPMT Education Services, and occasionally teaches in FPMT Dharma centers in Nepal and India.

ABOUT WISDOM PUBLICATIONS

Wisdom Publications is the leading publisher of contemporary and classic Buddhist books and practical works on mindfulness. Publishing books from all major Buddhist traditions, Wisdom is a nonprofit charitable organization dedicated to cultivating Buddhist voices the world over, advancing critical scholarship, and preserving and sharing Buddhist literary culture.

To learn more about us or to explore our other books, please visit our website at www.wisdompubs.org. You can subscribe to our eNewsletter, request a print catalog, and find out how you can help support Wisdom's mission either online or by writing to:

Wisdom Publications
199 Elm Street
Somerville, Massachusetts 02144 USA

You can also contact us at 617-776-7416 or info@wisdompubs.org.

Wisdom is a 501(c)(3) organization, and donations in support of our mission are tax deductible.

Wisdom Publications is affiliated with the Foundation for the Preservation of the Mahayana Tradition (FPMT).

MORE FROM WISDOM PUBLICATIONS

Essential Mind Training
Tibetan Classics, Volume One
Translated and introduced by Thupten Jinpa
296 pages | $16.95 | ebook $12.35

"Anyone intrigued by the potential to bend our minds in the direction of greater clarity and kindness will find great satisfaction in *Essential Mind Training*." —Daniel Goleman, author of *Emotional Intelligence*

The Essential Nectar
Meditations on the Buddhist Path
Geshe Rabten
Edited by Martin Willson
312 pages | $21.95 | ebook $10.20

Geshe Rabten's teachings reveal how we may see life's great value and, by taking up the profound practice described herein, make the most of its abundant opportunity.

Introduction to Tantra
The Transformation of Desire
Lama Thubten Yeshe
Edited by Jonathan Landaw, foreword by Philip Glass
192 pages | $16.95 | ebook $12.35

"The best introductory work on Tibetan Buddhist tantra available today."—Janet Gyatso, Harvard University

Transforming Problems into Happiness
Lama Zopa Rinpoche
Foreword by His Holiness the Dalai Lama
104 pages | $12.95 | ebook $9.43

"A masterfully brief statement of Buddhist teachings on the nature of humanity and human suffering. This book should be read as the words of a wise, loving parent."
—*Utne Reader*

Wisdom of the Kadam Masters
Tibetan Classics
Translated and introduced by Thupten Jinpa
232 pages | $16.95 | ebook $12.35

"*Wisdom of the Kadam Masters* shows how these pithy sayings from long ago offer anyone sound principles for living a meaningful, fulfilling, and happy life."—Daniel Goleman, author of *Emotional Intelligence*